KEY STAGE 3

• KEY STAGES IN HISTORY •

CW01043972

THE ERA OF THE SECOND WORLD WAR

R J Cootes L E Snellgrove

Nelson

Thomas Nelson and Sons Ltd
Nelson House   Mayfield Road
Walton-on-Thames   Surrey
KT12 5PL   UK

51 York Place
Edinburgh
EH1 3JD   UK

Nelson Blackie
Wester Cleddens Road
Bishopbriggs
Glasgow
G64 2NZ   UK

Thomas Nelson (Hong Kong) Ltd
Toppan Building 10/F
22A Westlands Road
Quarry Bay   Hong Kong

Thomas Nelson Australia
102 Dodds Street
South Melbourne
Victoria 3205   Australia

Nelson Canada
1120 Birchmount Road
Scarborough   Ontario
M1K 5G4   Canada

First published by Thomas Nelson and Sons Ltd 1994

ISBN 0-17-435065-1
NPN 9 8 7 6 5 4 3 2 1

Printed in Spain

Acknowledgements
The publishers are grateful to the following for the permission to
reproduce copyright material:
Aerofilm: p. 7; Archiv Fur Kunst: pp. 6,9 (bottom), 11, 13, 16, 17,
28, 30, 36, 49, 53 (bottom), 56, 58, 66, 74, 86, 93; Associated Press:
pp. 73, 101; Bettman: pp. 68, 69, 100; Bildarchiv: pp. 29, 37, 50;
J Allan Cash: pp. 88, 90 (left and right), 91 ; John Urling Clark:
pp. 85, 109; Commission des Communantes Europeennes: p. 115;
David King Collection: pp. 42 (top), 48; David Shepherd: p. 57;
Edimedia: p. 19; Ann Frank - Fonds, Basel: pp. 89, 90; Hulton
Deutsch: pp. 14, 18, 20 (top left), 21, 22, 24, 26, 34, 40, 42 (bottom),
44, 45, 53 (top), 54, 60 (inset), 63, 67, 71, 72, 80, 87, 89 (left), 103,
107, 108, 110, 111, 112 (top and bottom), 114, 116, 117; Imperial
War Museum: pp. 39, 52, 62, 64, 75, 77, 78, 81, 82; Paul Popper:
p. 84; Popperfoto: pp. 23, 38, 47, 60, 65, 76, 77 (inset), 79, 89 (right),
95, 105; Topham: p. 12; Ullstein Bilderdienst: pp. 9 (top), 32;
Weimar Archive: pp. 10, 27.

Preface

This book aims to provide a clear, coherent and interesting account for the majority of 13–14 year olds studying the relevant core unit of the National Curriculum. Great care has been taken to avoid elaborate language, complex sentence structures, obscure references and unexplained technical terms. At the same time, we have tried to guard against excessive brevity and over-simplification – common enemies of understanding. To allow adequate scope to explain ideas and concepts, and with Key Stage 3 assessment in mind, the basic text has been given a generous allocation of space.

Although we have adopted a thematic approach to the content, this is firmly set within a chronological framework. A detailed contents list and comprehensive index provide plenty of signposts through the book. Readers should be encouraged to make full use of both. For ease of reference, all the topics in the National Curriculum Orders are highlighted in bold type in the index.

Historical sources – both written and pictorial – are numbered consecutively in each chapter. However, to avoid cluttering the book with too many references, not all sources are keyed into the text. There are textual references to all the written sources, but only to those picture sources which directly support the narrative. The documentary extracts each carry a brief introduction to set them in context and all have been carefully edited and glossed. They have not been paraphrased, however, as we believe this would destroy their period flavour.

In selecting sources for the chapters on the war years we have focused on the impact of the fighting upon the lives of ordinary people – members of the armed forces and civilians on both sides.

The *Assessment Tasks* at the end of each chapter cover the Attainment Targets in a structured and balanced way, taking due account of the weighting of AT1. Many of the tasks lend themselves to either oral or written assignments. The additional groups of questions in the body of the text are designed to stimulate .both general discussion and clarification of historical terms and references. Many of these questions are also directly relevant to the Statements of Attainment.

We should like to thank our wives, Sarah and Jean, for their help, advice and forbearance.

R.J. Cootes
L.E. Snellgrove

Contents

The failed peace

The rise of Adolf Hitler

At the eleventh hour of the eleventh day of the eleventh month in 1918 the First World War ended when Germany admitted defeat. The Allies against Germany – Britain, France, Italy and the USA – had won. Along a battle-front of 900 miles in western Europe the guns fell silent and the killing stopped. A month before, senior German generals had told the Emperor, William II, that the army could no longer defend the country. A truce (temporary cease-fire) was arranged to prevent overwhelming numbers of Allied soldiers destroying the German army and invading Germany.

News of peace triggered off widespread changes in the government of Germany. William II fled abroad, and leading politicians set up a republic (a state without a monarchy) which hurriedly signed the truce. Two months later all men and women over twenty-one were given the vote in an election for a President and *Reichstag* (parliament).

Germany humbled

In May 1919 a peace conference assembled at Versailles near Paris in France. It was attended by representatives of all the victorious countries; German delegates were invited but took no part in the discussions. Amongst the 'Big Three' (Britain, France and the United States) there was disagreement about how Germany should be treated. The American President, Woodrow Wilson, wanted a peace which treated winners and losers fairly and equally. He also wanted to set up a permanent organisation, the League of Nations, to prevent wars in the future.

The British Prime Minister, David Lloyd George, represented a country which had lost nearly 1 million dead. The mood of his people was grim and bitter. 'Hang the Kaiser' (German Emperor) and 'Make Germany Pay' were popular slogans in Britain at the time. The French leader, Georges Clemenceau, hated the Germans. French losses were double those of Britain and large parts of France were a shell-scarred wilderness. He wanted to make sure Germany would never be strong enough to invade France again and inflict such suffering on its people.

SOURCE 1

Peacemaking, 1919. German delegates are forced to sign the First World War peace treaty in the Hall of Mirrors of the palace of Versailles, near Paris.

Some of the French who died in the First World War are buried in this vast cemetary near Verdun. In 1916, 350,000 were killed at Verdun in only four months' fighting. The building in the centre of the picture contains thousands of unidentified bones.

Europe After the First World War

On map:

Northern Schleswig to Denmark

Saar (controlled by the League of Nations until 1935)

Polish 'Corridor' & free city of Danzig

Alsace Lorraine to France

German losses in Treaty of Versailles, 1919

Rhineland 'demilitarised' zone

NB The lands given to Poland cut off the German territory of East Prussia from the rest of Germany

Consequently, although Wilson got his way in many matters, including the formation of the League of Nations, severe peace terms were imposed upon Germany **(Source 3)**. All its overseas possessions and the lands in Europe it had conquered in the previous 50 years were given to other countries. The army was cut to 100,000 men, the navy reduced and the air force destroyed. The Rhineland region of Germany, bordering France, was occupied by British and French troops and the Germans were forbidden to fortify it in any way (see map). This was to prevent Germany from using it as a springboard to attack France. The German Republic was ordered to pay reparations (compensation) to the Allies for damage done to France and Belgium during the fighting. The treaty clearly laid the blame for starting the war on Germany **(Source 4).**

Frances Stevenson was Lloyd George's secretary and, later, his wife. She went to the peace conference with him and kept a diary. Here is the entry for 7 May 1919.

P M (Lloyd George) went down to Versailles to present the Peace terms to the German delegates – a most beautiful spring day. I do not think David realised what an exhausting event it would be … The Germans were very arrogant and insolent … [Lloyd George] says it has made him more angry than any incident of the war, and if the Germans do not sign he will have no mercy on them. He says for the first time he has felt the same hatred for them that the French feel. I am rather glad they have stirred him up, so that he may keep stern with them to the end.

Harold Nicolson was a member of the British delegation to the Peace Conference. Twenty years later he had this to say about the Versailles Treaty.

The historian ... will come to the conclusion that we were very stupid men ... We came to Paris ... determined that a Peace of justice and wisdom should be negotiated; we left it, conscious that the treaties imposed upon our enemies were neither just nor wise.

SOURCE 5

Fritz Ernst was a German schoolboy in the period after the First World War. Looking back nearly fifty years later he explains how many Germans felt at the time.

In our high school in Stuttgart ... we believed that it was the stab in the back alone that had prevented a German victory ... We were taught to hate the French and British and to despise the Americans ... We were not meant to suspect that the ruling classes of Imperial Germany (the monarchy which fought the war) had made serious mistakes ... [Meanwhile] the Republic of which ... we were making fun was trying to pull the waggon out of the mud.

SOURCE 6

Here are two descriptions of Hitler during his days in Vienna, (a) by a friend, Reinhold Hanisch, who lived in the same hostel, and (b) by Hitler himself.

a On the very first day, there sat next to the bed that had been allotted to me a man who had nothing on except an old torn pair of trousers – Hitler. His clothes were being cleaned of lice, since for days he had been wandering about without a roof and in a terribly neglected condition.

b In the years 1909–10 I had so far improved my position that I no longer had to earn my daily bread as a manual labourer. I was now working independently as a draughtsman and painter in water-colours.

The German people were astonished and angry at these terms. They too had lost millions of men in the war, which they believed had been forced upon them. Now they were being punished whilst the men who had led them to war lived in comfortable retirement. Some began to claim that German troops had not been defeated fairly but had been 'stabbed in the back' by 'Jewish conspirators' and striking workers within Germany **(Source 5)**. One man who said this was an ex-soldier named Adolf Hitler.

Hitler's early years

Hitler was born in Austria on 20 April 1889, the son of a customs official. After leaving school he tried to become an art student but the Vienna Academy of Art turned him down. For several years he earned a living painting and selling his own postcards. He made very little money and lived in a men's hostel with down-and-outs **(Source 6)**. Other men in the hostel remembered him as lazy and moody.

In those days Austria was the centre of a large empire covering much of central Europe, including what is now Hungary, Slovakia, and the Czech Republic. In Vienna, the capital, lived Germans, Jews, Hungarians, Poles and Czechs. Austrians spoke German and Hitler thought of himself as a German. He looked down on other nationalities as 'inferior' and referred to Germans as 'the master race'. Like many Viennese, he hated Jews. Not only did he claim that they were evil and greedy but he was sure that rich and powerful Jews were plotting to take over the world.

When the First World War broke out in 1914 Hitler crossed into Germany and joined a German regiment. He fought in Belgium and France, was wounded and won the Iron Cross, a high award for bravery. Hitler found the comradeship and excitement of warfare more enjoyable than his lonely, dreary life in Vienna. He was in

QUESTIONS

1. In Source 6, which account is likely to be the more accurate, and why?

2. What was Hitler's main reason for hating the post-war republican government of Germany?

3. What impression of Lenin was the sculptor of Source 8 trying to give?

4. Why did Karl Marx believe that, in the long run, a revolution of the working classes could not be avoided?

hospital when the war ended, recovering from being gassed at the battle-front. When he heard the news of the German defeat, he said, 'Everything went black ... and I staggered back to my ward and buried my aching head between the blankets and pillow'. He condemned the German representatives who had signed the Versailles treaty as traitors and criminals.

Hitler left the army with the rank of corporal and went to Munich, capital of the German state of Bavaria. It was a good choice from his point of view. The Bavarian authorities despised the new German government and took as little notice as possible of its laws. When Hitler started making speeches attacking the Republic's ministers for agreeing to the peace settlement and co-operating with the Allies, they took no action. In peaceful times a person who stood on beerhall tables, shouting insults at Jews and calling government ministers traitors, would have been locked up. But these were not peaceful times. Munich was a violent city in which countless murders were committed by political gangs. People who denounced the Versailles treaty and talked of 'a stab in the back' in 1918 were popular.

Hitler (right) with fellow soldiers during the First World War. He called war 'the greatest of experiences'.

Hitler and the Communists

There was another reason why the authorities did not arrest Hitler. In his speeches he condemned Communists at a time when many people were afraid of the spread of their ideas. Only two years before, in 1917, a group of *Bolsheviks* (Communists) led by Vladimir Lenin had seized power in Russia. The Russian Tsar (Emperor), Nicholas II, had been murdered and a Communist state established.

Communists are followers of Karl Marx, a nineteenth-century German writer. According to Marx, all changes in society resulted from a struggle between the 'haves' and the 'have-nots'. These struggling groups he called *classes*. Marx argued that there was always a battle between *capitalists* – those who owned or

Statue of Vladimir Lenin, leader of Russia's Communist Revolution, in a Moscow square. The figures at the base are soldiers and workers.

In the *Manifesto of the Communist Party*, Karl Marx and his friend, Friedrich Engels, explained their aims.

The immediate aim of the Communists is … conquest of political power by the proletariat (workers) … The proletariat will use its political supremacy to take … all capital from the bourgeoisie (ruling class), to centralise all production in the hands of the state, by which we mean the proletariat organised as a ruling class … In the place of the old society, with its classes and class hatreds, we shall have an association, in which the free development of each [person] is the condition for the free development of all.

controlled the resources of industry and trade – and the *proletariat* (ordinary wage-earners) who lacked resources and whose lives were controlled by the capitalist class. Marx predicted that the down-trodden workers would eventually rise up, seize the resources of their countries and run them for the good of everybody **(Source 9)**. He called this system Communism because wealth would be owned in common and distributed evenly.

Owners of private property, from the richest capitalists to small shopkeepers and farmers, were against Communism. So were those who disliked drastic changes.

Many German factory workers, on the other hand, became Communists in the hope of a better life. There was even an unsuccessful Communist rising in Berlin, the German capital, in 1919. Personally, Hitler hated the Communist idea of all workers, regardless of their nationality, being 'comrades' and 'brothers'. To him, Germans were the 'master race'; he regarded German Communists as traitors who looked for help to Russia, a foreign power.

Lenin's success in turning Russia into a Communist state aroused the fears of the ruling classes throughout western Europe. Consequently, outspoken enemies of Communism, such as Hitler, were given plenty of encouragement. Hitler's rise to fame was swift. In 1919 he joined the German Workers' Party and soon made a name for himself as a speaker. Some people, when they listened to Hitler, thought he was mad. But throughout his career most Germans were fascinated by what he said and the way he said it.

In 1920 the Workers' Party joined another group, the National Socialist Workers' Party – the Nazis for short – and Hitler soon became their *Führer* (leader). The Nazis took as their badge the swastika, or crooked

Badges worn by various Nazi groups in the 1930s. The one top right was for young women members.

cross, and behaved more like an army than a political party. Nazi 'stormtroopers' wore uniforms, carried weapons and frequently beat up their opponents. Many were discontented youngsters looking for a fight, or unemployed ex-soldiers attracted by regular pay, clothing, food and lodgings. Such men enjoyed the comradeship of party rallies, with songs, speeches, slogans and flags.

The Beerhall Putsch

The Bavarian authorities allowed Hitler so much freedom that in 1923 he went too far. On 8 November he rushed into a Munich beerhall waving a revolver and shouted that he was going to overthrow the Republic. He called on his supporters to join him in a march on Berlin.

It seemed a good moment for a *Putsch* (rising). French troops had that year occupied the Ruhr industrial region of Germany because reparation payments were late. This invasion had caused widespread German resentment, with strikes and disruption in the Ruhr, and protest meetings elsewhere in Germany. However, Hitler had exaggerated his own importance. The Bavarian government and army leaders did dislike the Republic and the Communists. But they were not prepared to let the leader of a minor political party become ruler of Germany. The Nazi march was fired on by police who killed sixteen of Hitler's supporters. Hitler was arrested and charged with treason.

The 'Beerhall Putsch' should have marked the end of Hitler's political career. Instead, he became better known because his trial was reported throughout Germany. Hitler boasted of what he had done (**Source 11**) and the judge, who was on his side, allowed him to make long speeches which had nothing to do with the case. The Nazi leader was sentenced to five years in prison, but he served only nine months. He had such an easy time in prison that he was able to write a book, *Mein Kampf* (My Struggle), whilst he was there.

Mein Kampf is the story of Hitler's life. It

was also a plan for Germany's future. In it, Hitler made two promises. First, he said he would bring under German rule all European peoples who spoke German. This meant taking over Austria and a part of Czechoslovakia known as the Sudetenland. Second, he promised that he would conquer extra 'living space' for Germans in eastern Europe. These lands would be taken from Russia and Poland. People who read *Mein Kampf* often despised its bad grammar and dangerous ideas. Yet within twenty years Hitler made these promises come true.

'Hitler over Germany'

After 1923 Hitler decided that violent revolution was unlikely to succeed whilst

the army and police remained loyal to the state. So he made friends with the rich and powerful and used their money and influence to build a political party strong enough to win elections.

Nazi election campaigns were run by a clever journalist named Joseph Goebbels. Goebbels made sure that films of Hitler and records of his speeches were widely available. He arranged radio broadcasts and plastered the walls of German cities with posters promising work and prosperity if Hitler came to power. During elections Hitler often travelled to meetings by aeroplane, so Goebbels named one campaign 'Hitler over Germany'. Aircraft were still a novelty in those days, so the arrival of the Nazi leader's plane, usually caught in a cluster of searchlights at night, and his dramatic appearance in a spotlight on the platform, roused the waiting crowd of supporters to a frenzy.

The Nazis did best when times were bad because this made people want a change of government. Their big chance came in 1929 when a falling-off in world trade meant that industrial countries found it hard to sell their products and unemployment rose. This trade depression, starting in the United States, hit Germany particularly hard. The investment of American money had been helping German industry to recover after the war. Once the flow of American dollars stopped businesses collapsed and factories shut down. People from all walks of life – farmers, shopkeepers, industrial workers – found themselves out of work. Between 1929 and 1933 the number of jobless rose from 1.3 to 6 million **(Source 14)**. In their distress, most people blamed the government and both the Nazis and Communists tried to take advantage of its difficulties.

SOURCE 13

In this Nazi poster, *Deutschland* (Germany) is shown as a woman clinging on to Hitler. The words on the flag translate as Loyalty, Honour and Order.

SOURCE 14

Some of the anger and despair felt by Germans during the depression comes out in this extract from a book written by a Nazi, Kurt Ludecke. He is referring to the time just before Hitler came to power.

And what of Germany? Swarming with unemployed, now nearly six million of them, cheated by ... gangsters, but alive with the determination of youth. All over the land, young spirits were rearing up in ... protest against the wretchedness of a life that their fathers seemed to have spoiled for them. This was the generation which had grown up during the war ... Whether they marched with the Nazis, as they did in increasing numbers, or shouted the battle-cry of the Communists, they were resolved on change, on a new order.

Unemployed workers in the German city of Hanover queue for their 'dole' money during the depression of the early 1930s. Notice the Nazi slogan on a wall.

QUESTIONS

1 Hitler said the Beerhall Putsch was 'the greatest piece of good fortune' in his life. Can you explain why?

2 What does Source 11 tell us about Hitler's attitude towards the law?

3 Why did many young Germans believe that their fathers had spoilt their lives (Source 14)?

4 When Hitler became Chancellor, why do you think he asked the voters to give him power for only four years?

SOURCE 16

Christopher Isherwood was an English writer who lived in Berlin in the early 1930s. He describes the background against which Hitler came to power.

Berlin was in a state of civil war. Hate exploded suddenly, without warning, out of nowhere; at street corners, in restaurants, cinemas, dance-halls, swimming baths; at midnight, after breakfast, in the middle of the afternoon. Knives were whipped out, blows were dealt with spiked rings, beer-mugs, chair-legs ... In the middle of the street a young man would be attacked, stripped, thrashed and left bleeding on the pavement; in fifteen seconds it was all over ... The newspapers were full of death-bed photographs of rival supporters, Nazi and ... Communist.

In this crisis Hitler's message was straightforward. He would give work to all, defy the Versailles treaty and end the Communist 'menace'. Disorder grew worse with street battles between Nazi and Communist gangs **(Source 16)**. A series of elections showed that support for the Nazis was growing. However, no political party could obtain an outright majority in the Reichstag (parliament). Between elections the country was run by a Chancellor (Prime Minister) assisted by ministers from several parties.

In these circumstances the man who had the final say in forming governments was the President, an elderly general named Paul von Hindenberg. Under the laws of the Republic, the President could appoint a new Chancellor if he considered the country to be in danger in any way. Hindenberg did not like Hitler whom he thought 'a queer fellow'. But, as the crisis deepened, Hindenberg's advisers suggested that the best way to satisfy the Nazis and crush the Communists was to give Hitler a post in the government. On 30 January 1933 Hindenberg made Hitler Chancellor.

The Reichstag fire

Hitler's first act as Chancellor was to call an election to choose a new Reichstag.

Publicly, he asked for four years of power. In private he boasted that if the Nazis won there would be no more elections for a hundred years!

A week before polling day the Reichstag building in Berlin caught fire. The Nazis at once blamed the Communists who, they claimed, intended the fire as a signal for revolt. The Communists blamed the Nazis. Although a Dutch Communist, Marinus van der Lubbe, was found inside the burning building with firelighters in his pocket, it now seems likely that there was no Communist plot and van der Lubbe started the blaze on his own. Whatever the truth, public alarm at the fire helped swing voting the Nazis' way. They polled 43 per cent of the total vote, and this, added to the 8 per cent won by their allies, the Nationalists, gave them the majority they needed to rule Germany.

Hitler kept his word. There was never another free election while he lived. The Nazis banned all other political parties. They imprisoned, tortured and murdered anyone who opposed them. Even the Stormtroopers, who had fought the Nazis' street battles, were wiped out suddenly in 1934 when they seemed to be getting too powerful. Special laws were passed which took away all citizenship rights from Jews. A new force, the black-uniformed SS (*Schutz Staffel*, or protective squad) ran a secret police, the *Gestapo*, which terrorised opponents of the government. Communists, Jews and other groups such as gypsies whom the Nazis regarded as 'inferior' were imprisoned in concentration camps.

The majority of Germans approved of Hitler's rule after years of disorder and uncertainty. They liked his talk of making Germany great again and defying the terms of the Versailles treaty **(Source 18)**. They were pleased when the Nazi policy of building a new, powerful army, navy and air force gave plenty of work. Only a few thoughtful people were worried where this attempt to reverse the result of the First World War might lead.

SOURCE 17

The burning Reichstag building on 27 February 1933. Next day, before there had been any investigation, Hitler persuaded President Hindenberg to ban all personal freedoms in case of a Communist rising.

SOURCE 18

Christopher Isherwood (see page 13) explains how many ordinary German citizens felt about the Nazis.

They smiled approvingly at these youngsters in their big, swaggering boots who were going to upset the Treaty of Versailles. They were pleased ... because Hitler had promised to protect the small tradesman, because their newspapers told them the good times were coming ... And they were thrilled with secret pleasure, like schoolboys, because the Jews, their business rivals, and the Marxists (Communists) ... had been found guilty of the [1918] defeat ... and were going to catch it.

Assessment tasks

A Knowledge and understanding

1 a Describe the different attitudes of Britain, France and the United States towards the Treaty of Versailles.

  b How might these attitudes have been influenced by the war experiences of each country?

2 Here are some possible reasons for Hitler's rise to power.
- The Beerhall Putsch, 1923
- Fear of Communism
- Germany's defeat in the First World War
- The Reichstag fire, 1933
- The terms of the Treaty of Versailles
- Rising unemployment

  a Which do you think was the single most important, and why?

  b Put the remainder in what you consider to be their order of importance, giving reasons for your answer.

3 a What have you learned from this chapter and its sources about life in Germany in the 1920s and 1930s?

  b What connections can you find between ordinary people's lives and the political events of the period?

B Interpretations and sources

4 Here are two contrasting views about the reparations Germany had to pay after the First World War. *A milliard* is a thousand millions.

> From 1936 onward she (Germany) will have to pay us three billion, two hundred and fifty million dollars annually to keep pace with the interest alone. At the end of any year in which she pays less than this sum she will owe more than she did at the beginning of it. And if she is to discharge (pay off) the capital sum in thirty years from 1936 ... she must pay an additional six hundred and fifty million dollars annually ... It is my judgement ... that Germany cannot pay anything approaching this sum.
> (John Maynard Keynes, 1920)

> Had they (reparations) been ... enforced, they would no doubt have put the screw on Germany ... Reparations were not paid because Germany ... did not want to pay them, and the Allies showed themselves incapable or unwilling to take jointly the necessary measures which could have made Germany pay ... Mr Keynes predicted that in the next thirty years Germany could not possibly be expected to pay more than 2 milliard marks in reparation. In the six years preceding September 1939 Germany ... spent on rearmament alone about seven times as much.
> (Etienne Mantoux, 1952)

  a What are the main differences between these two accounts?

  b The first writer is English, the second French. How might this help to explain their disagreement?

5 a How does Source 16 help to explain the attitudes of the Germans described in Source 18?

  b In what ways do Christopher Isherwood's observations help us to understand Hitler's rise to power?

  c Could there be any reason to question the reliability of Isherwood as a source?

6 Look carefully at Source 13.

  a How does it help to explain the 'message' Hitler was trying to get across to the German people?

  b How useful is this source in explaining Hitler's growing popularity compared with the written sources in the chapter?

Stalin and Mussolini

Communism, Fascism and democracy in the 1930s

In August 1935 officials of the Russian Communist Party arranged for Alexei Stakhanov, a miner, to cut some easy coal-seams. He was given the best equipment and experienced assistants. In 5 hours 45 minutes Stakhanov cut 102 tonnes of coal – fourteen times the usual amount produced per shift. The government was delighted. Stakhanov became a national hero. He was given medals, cash prizes and seaside holidays with his family. 'Stakhanovite' became the name of a movement aimed at increasing industrial production in Russia.

Stakhanov's record showed up the low level of output in Russian coal-mines at the time. But it encouraged other industries to find their own 'Stakhanovites' and so helped to increase output throughout the country. Moreover, because Stakhanov's output that day was declared 'normal' by the government, workers who could not equal it were paid less.

Five Year Plans

The Stakhanovite movement arose from far-reaching plans to modernise Russia after the revolution (see page 9). Soviet Russia – so called because the Communists ruled through workers' councils called Soviets – was backward when Lenin died in 1924. Farming was primitive, producing hardly enough to feed the people, and there were few modern, well-equipped industries. Lenin's successor, Josef Stalin, was convinced that one day Communist Russia would be attacked by its capitalist neighbours. Therefore modern industries would be needed to supply the Soviet armed forces in their struggle with well-equipped Western armies (**Source 2**).

Stalin's industrialisation programme involved a series of Five Year Plans, each setting production targets for coal, iron, timber, electricity, steel, concrete and tractors. To achieve these aims, Stalin's government hired foreign engineers and bought the best foreign machinery. He was sure Russia had no time to lose, so he insisted that the Five Year Plans were completed in only four years! Stalin's officials toured the country, often setting workers impossible targets.

Industrial progress was impressive. The first Five Year Plan created 90 new towns, including a steel centre at Magnitogorsk (**Source 3**) and motor vehicle factories at Gorki and Rostov. Canals, railways and dams for electric power turned areas of open countryside into industrial centres. Some men and women went to work on

Josef Stalin (1879–1953). The son of a shoemaker, he first trained as a priest. He gave himself the name Stalin which is Russian for 'Man of steel'.

these projects because they were hungry but most were forced to leave their homes and work where directed. Discipline was harsh. If workers failed to reach their targets their wages were reduced. If they missed a day's work they were sacked. When unwilling or unskilled workers produced defective goods, the authorities claimed such mistakes were deliberate. Many of the accused were shot. Foreign experts thought guilty of 'sabotage' were expelled, often after a public trial.

Although each Plan promised people a better standard of living, there was little attempt to produce goods the people wanted. Industrial machinery, tractors or arms for defence came before clothes, furniture, radios or private cars. A riddle became popular: 'Why were Adam and Eve like Soviet citizens? Because they lived in Paradise and had nothing to wear!'

Collectivisation

The growth of industry meant extra food was needed for the new army of factory workers. This could only be produced by more efficient farming methods. Lenin had taken the large estates from the landowners and distributed the land amongst the peasants. Stalin believed that farming output would be increased if peasants pooled both their land and livestock and shared their work and profits in 'collective' farms.

SOURCE 3

Factory building at Magnitogorsk in the Ural mountains (1932). Two or three years earlier this had been open countryside.

SOURCE 2

Stalin defended his policy of hurried industrial development in a speech in 1931.

It is sometimes asked whether it is not possible to slow down the tempo a bit … No, comrades, it is not possible … Now that we have overthrown capitalism and power is in the hands of the working class … we will defend [Russia's] independence … [We] must put an end to its backwardness in the shortest possible time … There is no other way … We are fifty or a hundred years behind the advanced countries. We must make good this gap in ten years. Either we do it, or they crush us.

QUESTIONS

1 Why did Stalin expect to be attacked by the countries of Western Europe?

2 Why was Soviet Russia slow to produce goods the people wanted?

3 Can you think why Russian peasants were so opposed to working on collective farms?

4 In Source 6, why do you think the Communist in the train denied that there was a famine?

SOURCE 4

In his novel, *Virgin Soil Upturned*, a Russian writer, Mikhail Sholokhov, described what happened in one village about to be collectivised.

Men began slaughtering their cattle every night at Gremyachy. As soon as it grew dusk, one could hear the muffled bleating of the sheep, the death squeal of a pig piercing the stillness, the whimper of a calf. Both the peasants who had joined the collective farm and the individual farmers killed off their stock … In two nights the number of cattle in Gremyachy was halved … [Everybody was saying] 'Kill, it's not ours now! Kill, the state butchers will do it if we don't! Kill, they won't give you meat to eat in the collective farm.'

SOURCE 5

This painting shows workers threshing corn on a collective farm. People looking at it might have been misled into thinking that Russian peasants willingly accepted the 'collectivisation' of farming.

This collectivisation of farming caused bitter resentment. Peasants killed their livestock rather than join a collective **(Source 4)** and often murdered officials sent to supervise the changeover. Stalin sent all who resisted to labour (prison) camps. Altogether 5 million peasants were expelled from their homes and driven to barren regions where most died of starvation or cold. Some rebellious villages were attacked by troops or bombed from the air.

After years of disruption and misery, Stalin got his way. But the results were the opposite of what he had hoped. Food production dropped disastrously during the early 1930s as livestock were slaughtered and fields left unworked. Food became scarce and famine killed millions **(Source 6)**. It was many years before the new Soviet agriculture yielded the amount of food that had been grown before collectivisation.

Stalin's Terror

When Lenin seized power in 1917 (see page 9) he realised that the Communists had only limited support; the majority of the population were frightened into obedience. Communist policies, such as *nationalisation* (industry taken over by the state), were applied ruthlessly. A new secret police, the *Cheka*, imprisoned, tortured or shot all opponents of the government. Under Stalin, such sinister police methods became part of the Soviet way of life.

At first, Stalin shared power with other leaders. Gradually, however, he became sole ruler, putting his own supporters in jobs at all levels of government. By 1929 he was powerful enough to sack his colleagues after accusing them of disloyalty. These quarrels were made more bitter by disagreements about Russia's future. Some Communist Party leaders believed the Russian revolution would fail unless it spread to other countries. Stalin thought that the ruling classes of capitalist states were too powerful to be overthrown, although he employed agents to try to weaken them. In place of ideas of 'world revolution' Stalin took as his slogan, 'Socialism (meaning Communism) in one state'.

SOURCE 6

In March 1932 Gareth Jones, a British visitor to Russia, reported on the famine gripping the country as a result of the battle over collectivisation.

I walked alone through villages and twelve collective farms. Everywhere was the cry, 'There is no bread; we are dying' ... In a train a Communist denied to me that there was a famine. I flung into the spittoon a crust of bread I had been eating from my own supply. The peasant, my fellow passenger, fished it out and ate it. I threw orange peel into the spittoon. The peasant again grabbed and devoured (ate) it.

The rise of Nazi Germany roused deep fears in Stalin's suspicious nature. Hitler made no secret of his hatred of Communism and his contempt for Russians as 'inferior'. What if the Nazi leader persuaded traitors inside Russia to disrupt industry and overthrow the government? Stalin now became even more ruthless in stamping out opposition. During the 1930s his old colleagues were accused of 'crimes against the state'. Most of them confessed after torture, long imprisonment and threats to their families.

Between 1934 and 1938, seventeen leaders of the 1917 Revolution, half the Communist Party General Committee, 23 generals and eight admirals were shot after *show trials* – so called because there was never any doubt of the verdict. A terrible fear gripped Russia as more and more 'plots' were uncovered. To save their own skins, people informed against their neighbours, workmates, even friends and relatives **(Source 8)**. Many thousands were executed or sent to labour camps **(Source 9)**. Sometimes, the entire staff of a factory, office or shop would vanish overnight .

The rise of Fascism

The victory of the revolutionaries in Russia and the distress and turmoil left by the First World War caused millions of Europeans to turn to Communism. In Germany, as we have seen, Communists were numerous enough to try to seize power in 1919. In Italy the growth of Communist power led to a violent reaction.

Italy emerged from the First World War with a grievance. The Italians had joined in the war against Germany when they were promised territories ruled by Austria, the Germans' ally. At Versailles, however, President Wilson rejected Italian claims because they had been contained in a secret treaty. He blamed secret treaties for leading to misunderstandings which had helped cause the war in the first place. The Italians were disappointed and angry; in some towns Wilson's portrait was torn down or decorated with a German helmet!

SOURCE 8

Nadezdha Mandelstam describes life in Stalin's Russia. Her husband, a writer who dared to criticise the Soviet dictator, died in a labour camp in 1938.

As regards the Stalinist terror ... that it might end – this we could never imagine. What reason was there for it to end? Everybody ... went smilingly about the business of carrying out instructions. It was essential to smile – if you didn't it meant you were discontented ... The mask was taken off only at home, and then not always – even from the children you had to conceal how horror-struck you were; otherwise, God save you, they might let something slip at school.

SOURCE 9

By 1938, nine million people were prisoners in Soviet labour camps. This description by a survivor shows what inmates could expect.

In the middle of a deserted, muddy plot of land, surrounded by a fence with guard towers at each corner, there stood cages into which groups of men were put when they arrived. The prisoners' barracks could not hold more than twenty per cent of the prisoners. The others wallowed in the mud, exposed to the cold and rain. They lit fires, pulling the barracks apart for wood. Now and then the club-swinging guards chased the men from one cage to another, hitting them ... without any reason. Twice a day the prisoners received one third of a litre of soup, and once a day about half a kilo of bread. Drinking water was drawn from canals, ditches and puddles.

Benito Mussolini, pictured around 1920 at the start of his political career. From the first he preferred to use force to settle arguments. He once led a march on a town hall and threatened to throw the mayor out of the window if the price of milk was not reduced.

Italy had emerged from the First World War deeply in debt and with millions of unemployed. Communist ideas had spread like wildfire; in September 1920 half a million workers went on strike and occupied their factories. The Fascists declared 'war' on such activity. This gave them the support of the ruling classes – wealthy landowners and industrialists, the middle classes and richer peasants. As the situation worsened, the Fascists, or *blackshirts* (so-called from the colour of their uniforms) set out to 'restore order'. Street battles between Communists and blackshirts became commonplace. Men were beaten to death, filled with castor oil or made to eat live toads. In three years 3000 people were killed.

One man who took advantage of these grievances was Benito Mussolini. Mussolini was a journalist with a violent nature and a gift for words. He returned from the army after the war convinced that what his country needed was rule by 'a man who is ruthless and energetic enough to make a clean sweep'. Such a man would 'dictate' policy, choosing 'superior men' to help him. Italy's democratically elected government would be swept away by such a 'dictator'. In 1919 Mussolini founded the *Fasci di Combattimento* (Fighting Group). They boasted that they were bound together as tightly as the bundle of rods and axes, the *fascinae*, which had been the symbol of power in Ancient Rome. His supporters became known as 'Fascists' for short **(Source 11)**.

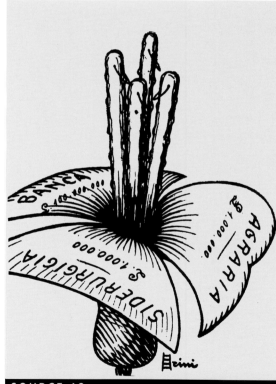

SOURCE 12

How an artist saw Italian Fascism. The stem of the 'flower' is the party, represented by heavy, studded clubs. The petals represent Fascism's supporters: bankers, the owners of industry and wealthy farmers.

SOURCE 11

In the summer of 1933, soon after Hitler came to power, a German diplomat went to Italy to see Mussolini. Here he compares the two dictators.

I found the Italian dictator a very different man from Hitler. Short in stature, but with an air of great authority, his massive head gave an impression of great strength of character. He handled people like a man used to having his orders obeyed, but displayed immense charm … Hitler always has a slight air of uncertainty, as though feeling his way, whereas Mussolini was calm, dignified and appeared the complete master of whatever subject was being discussed … He spoke excellent French and German.

Mussolini (second from the left) with some of his Fascist followers during the March on Rome, 28 October 1922.

In 1922 Mussolini organised a march of his supporters on Rome, the Italian capital, to destroy the power of the Communists once and for all. When the Fascist columns were still 40 miles from the city, Victor Emmanuel, the King of Italy, ordered the army and police not to resist; he was convinced the Fascists were the best defence against Communism. Mussolini was made Prime Minister of a government with representatives of all political parties.

For two years Mussolini ruled within the law. Then his grip tightened. Opposition parties were banned and the press censored. Parliament lost its power to make laws and workers the right to strike. Mussolini became more than a Prime Minister. He became 'Il Duce' (the leader) who wore military uniform in public and made speeches glorifying war **(Source 14)**. His portrait and the slogan 'Mussolini is always right' were hung from public buildings. Italians were promised that they would conquer not only the territories denied them at Versailles but a new 'Roman Empire' in North Africa.

QUESTIONS

1 What was the attraction of Mussolini to many Italians?

2 King Victor Emmanuel had reason to regret his support for Mussolini in 1922. Can you explain why?

3 Can you think why Mussolini referred to Italy's African conquests as a 'Roman' empire?

4 Why were the French in particular alarmed by the USA's refusal to join the League of Nations?

SOURCE 14

Fascist slogans like these were often chanted at meetings of Mussolini and his supporters.

A minute on the battlefield is worth a lifetime of peace!

War is to the male what child-bearing is to the female!

Believe! Obey! Fight!

He who has steel has bread!

Nothing has ever been won in history without bloodshed!

Better to live one day like a lion than a hundred years like a sheep!

The failure of collective security

By 1935 three major European powers – Germany, Russia and Italy – were one-party states ruled by dictators. Britain and France, on the other hand, remained democracies in which governments were freely elected at regular intervals by most adults. These governments had to take account of public opinion. In a democracy decisions are taken after discussion and debate. Dictators, however, make decisions fast and act swiftly because they ignore public opinion and crush protest. For this reason, British and French politicians found it increasingly difficult to deal with Hitler and Mussolini.

French policy was dominated by fear of Germany. The French had a smaller population than the Germans and nowhere near the industrial power. At the Versailles peace conference their hopes of security had rested on a settlement backed by the power of the United States and the League of Nations. Under the terms of the League's Charter, if a member state was attacked by an aggressor the other members would come to its aid. This scheme was called *collective security*. Unfortunately, such a plan had been upset almost immediately when the US Congress (parliament) refused to sign the treaty or join the League. This was because most Americans did not want to be involved in Europe's troublesome affairs.

Congress's decision was a deep disappointment to President Wilson who had pinned his hopes of world peace on the League. Without the United States, the arrangements made at the peace conference fell apart and France was left to face Germany without such powerful support. The French responded by trying to keep Germany weak. They insisted that reparations should be paid regularly and that the neighbouring Rhineland region of Germany should be *demilitarised* (kept free of weapons and soldiers) **(Source 15)**. The French tried to make sure that Germany's total armed forces remained small. They also formed alliances with countries to the east of Germany – Yugoslavia, Romania, Czechoslovakia and Poland – in the hope that these smaller states would join France in any future conflict. Meanwhile the French built a massive fortification, the Maginot Line, along their border with Germany **(Source 16)**.

SOURCE 15

In these notes, André Tardieu, a French representative at the peace conference in 1919, explains the importance of the demilitarisation of the Rhineland to France.

For France, as for Great Britain and the United States, it is necessary to create a zone of safety [against Germany] ... This zone the naval powers (Britain and the USA) created by their fleets and the elimination of the German fleets ... This zone, France ... unable to eliminate the millions of Germans trained for war, must create by the Rhine, by an inter-allied [military] occupation ... If she did not do so, she would once more be exposed ... [to] an enemy invasion ... France does not demand for herself the left bank of the Rhine ... only an inter-allied occupation of it.

SOURCE 16

One of the guns built into the Maginot Line – the huge steel and concrete fortification defending France's eastern frontier. It was named after the French Minister of War at the time.

When Hitler came to power the position of France grew much more dangerous. Within months, the Nazi dictator had taken Germany out of the League of Nations because, so he claimed, only Germany and not the Allies had disarmed after the war. Reparation payments (see page 7) had already stopped because of the trade depression and Germany had begun to rearm secretly. A stronger Germany meant that France's small, eastern European allies would stand little chance in a war. Reluctantly, the French took advantage of Stalin's fear of Germany to sign a five-year alliance with Russia (1935).

It was not surprising that nations were now ignoring the League. In 1931 it had faced its first big test and failed when Japanese troops invaded the Chinese province of Manchuria. Both China and Japan were members of the League. However, Russia, the only country with a land border with Manchuria, was not a member. The League was able to do little except protest at the Japanese aggression and send a team to investigate the fighting. When this commission condemned the invasion, Japan left the League. By 1932 the Japanese had occupied the whole of Manchuria.

Abyssinia and the Rhineland

In 1935 Mussolini invaded Abyssinia (now Ethiopia) as part of his plan to create an Italian empire in Africa. Although his action was condemned by the League of Nations, Britain and France at first entered into secret talks designed to give part of Abyssinia to Italy. When this became known in Britain there was uproar, for many people demanded that Italy should obey the League and stop the aggression.

The British government was now forced to take a tougher line. It persuaded the League to put sanctions (a ban) on key supplies to Italy, with the intention of crippling its war effort. However as oil, the most vital commodity for modern war, was not banned, these sanctions were

ineffective. The only result was to enrage the Italian people and drive Mussolini into a close alliance with Hitler. In 1936, after

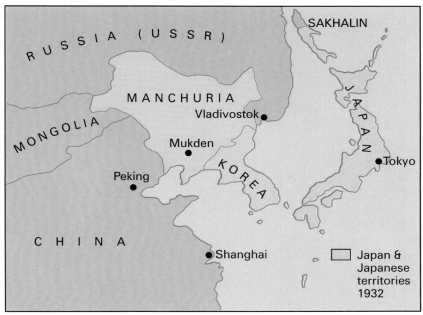

Japanese Occupation of Manchuria, 1932

Italian Fascist forces at the Red Sea port of Massawa during the invasion of Abyssinia (1935).

German troops crossing a bridge over the river Rhine to enter the city of Cologne in March 1936. Hitler later admitted, 'The 48 hours after the march into the Rhineland were the most nerve-wracking of my life'.

sanctions had been dropped and Abyssinia conquered, Italy and Germany signed an alliance called the Rome-Berlin Axis.

With the world distracted by the Abyssinian crisis, in 1936 Hitler made his first move against the Versailles treaty. He sent his troops to re-occupy the German Rhineland which had been 'demilitarised' by the terms of the peace settlement (see page 22). His excuse was that the new French-Soviet alliance was a threat to Germany. Since he knew his action might lead to war Hitler ordered his men to retreat if attacked by the French. He need not have worried. The French government had no desire for war and neither had its generals; they sent back reports exaggerating the numbers of German troops. France did nothing, even though Hitler's action cut it off from its allies in the east.

During this crisis the French were not supported by Britain. Certain British politicians said openly that the Germans were entitled to go 'into their own backyard'. The Rhineland was, after all, German territory. In any case, the British government had decided that as the Versailles treaty was unfair to Germany and collective security had failed, the time had come to deal directly with Hitler.

Two days after the re-occupation of the Rhineland by German troops, Hitler said this in a speech at Breslau.

Not we alone, the conquered of yesterday, but also the victors ... [know] that something was not as it should be ... Peoples must find a new relation to each other ... But they make a mistake who think that ... over this new order ... can stand the word 'Versailles'. That would be, not the foundation stone of the new order, but its gravestone.

Assessment tasks

A Knowledge and understanding

1 In what ways did the Communist reforms in Russia (i) make the country stronger, and (ii) make life harder for many people?

2 a What factors led many Italians to support the rise of Fascism?

b In what ways were political attitudes in Italy similar to those in Germany after the First World War?

3 Here are some reasons why the League of Nations failed to achieve its aims:

- The USA did not become a member.
- The League lacked the power to enforce its will.
- Nazi Germany withdrew from the League.
- Italy was not stopped from attacking Abyssinia.
- Britain's leaders thought the 1919 peace settlement was hard on Germany.

a Arrange these reasons in what you consider to be their order of importance, and explain your answer.

b In what ways are these different reasons connected?

B Interpretations and sources

4 John Scott was an American engineer who worked at Magnitogorsk, a steel-making town in the Ural mountains. Hewlett Johnson was an English clergyman who visited Communist Russia.

In early April it was still bitter cold ... everything was frozen solid. By May the ground had thawed and the city was swimming in mud ... Welding became next to impossible as our ragged cables short-circuited at every step ... Plague had broken out not far away ... The resistance of the population [to disease] was low because of undernourishment ... and overwork. Sanitary conditions were appalling ... In the barracks we were consumed by bed-bugs and other vermin ... Three-quarters [of the population] came seeking work, bread cards, better conditions. The rest came under compulsion.
(John Scott, 1942)

In 1929 ... herds of cattle browsed on the slope of the [Magnet] mountain. Today one of the world's supreme steel centres hums and roars ... The Magnet mountain gives its name to Magnitogorsk ... Workers of thirty-five nationalities assembled and built barracks for workers, settlements for foreign specialists, cooperative stores, restaurants, hospitals, nurseries, clubs and a theatre ... The city itself is planned with care ... [with] seventeen blocks of buildings, each with its own department store, schools ...; each apartment in the block of flats with its own bath, running water, electric light, gas and central heating.
(Hewlett Johnson, 1939)

a Can you think of reasons which might explain why these accounts are so different?

b Which account do you think the workers in Magnitogorsk would have found closer to their experience, and why?

5 a How do Sources 4, 6, 8 and 9 help us to build up a picture of life in Soviet Russia?

b Do you think these sources are all equally reliable? Give reasons for your answer.

6 Compare the usefulness of Sources 12 and 14. Which tells you more about Fascism, and why?

3 The road to war

Europe in the 1930s

Hardly were German troops settled in the Rhineland than a fresh dispute sent shock waves across Europe. In July 1936 army officers, led by General Francisco Franco, rebelled against the elected government of Spain.

Civil war in Spain

The Spanish Civil War arose out of long-standing grievances caused by poverty and bad government. Like France, Spain was a republic – the King had been forced to leave the country in 1931. In February 1936 a new republican government was elected which proposed far-reaching changes to reduce poverty and give ordinary people a fairer share of the country's wealth. Although this government had few Communist members, General Franco claimed its real aim was to create a Communist state. Many of Franco's supporters were Fascists. Republican leaders condemned Franco as yet another Fascist dictator in the making.

With Fascists on one side and Communists on the other it was easy for foreigners to misunderstand the true causes of the war. Men of many nationalities who detested fascist ideas and were tired of their bullying rushed to Spain to 'do something' about it by fighting for the Republic. They formed 'International Brigades' which played a key role in the major battles of the war. On the other side, some decided that Franco was leading a 'crusade' against Communism and joined his forces.

It was the reaction of Hitler, Mussolini

SOURCE 1

General Franco is proclaimed leader of Spain by his supporters (October 1936). Franco won the Spanish Civil War and ruled Spain until his death in 1975.

SOURCE 2

Hitler's Foreign Minister, Joachim von Ribbentrop, describes a meeting with his master soon after the start of the Spanish Civil War.

The Führer … explained that Germany would not tolerate a Communist Spain … The Führer said … 'If Spain goes Communist, France … will also … in due course and then Germany is finished. Wedged between the powerful Soviet bloc in the East and a strong Communist French-Spanish bloc in the West, we could hardly do anything if Moscow (Russia) chose to attack us.

SOURCE 3

Italian troops in Spain during the Civil War march past General Franco. They were heavily defeated at Guadalajara by the Republican army assisted by International Brigades – the first time Fascists were beaten in battle.

and Stalin which eventually turned the war into a struggle between Communism and Fascism. Hitler responded to Franco's appeal for help by sending money, weapons and a squadron of bombers to the rebels **(Source 2)**. Meanwhile Mussolini sent 50,000 troops. The Republic turned to Stalin for aid and he sent supplies in return for Spain's entire stock of gold. He also sent agents to help him gain control in the Republican-held territory **(Source 4)**. This policy failed when Franco won the war in March 1939.

The French government wanted Franco to be beaten. But they were afraid to get too deeply involved because of the threat from Germany. As a result, France was half-hearted in its support for the Republic, sometimes sending aid and at other times cutting it off. The Conservative government in Britain took a different view. It was strongly against Communism, but it was also worried in case the conflict in Spain widened into another world war. With this in mind, Britain suggested that all states should refuse to help either side – a policy of non-intervention. In September 1936 a Non-Intervention Committee met in London but, as many of its members were openly helping one side or the other, it proved ineffective.

The Spanish Civil War was a 'dress rehearsal' for the Second World War, not only as a battle between democracy and dictatorship, Fascism and Communism, but also in the way it was fought. With its tank battles, mass bombing of cities, its refugees, radio propaganda and huge casualties, it showed the world what was to come **(Source 5)**.

SOURCE 4

Here one of Stalin's undercover agents explains why the Soviet dictator sent aid to the Spanish Republican government.

The world believed that Stalin's actions in Spain were in some way connected with world [Communist] revolution. But this is not true. Stalin believed it possible to create in Spain a regime (government) controlled by him; that done he could command the respect of France and England, win from them the offer of a real alliance and either accept it … [or use it] as a bargaining point to arrive at a compact (agreement) with Germany.

SOURCE 5

The Germans sent a squadron of aircraft to Spain to practise bombing techniques. In April 1937 they destroyed the small town of Guernica, killing 1654 people. Here, a Spanish priest describes the raid.

I arrived at Guernica on April 26th at 4.40pm. I had hardly left the car when the bombardment began. The people were terrified. They fled, abandoning their livestock in the market place. The bombardment lasted until 7.45. During that time five minutes did not elapse without the skies being black with German planes. The planes descended very low, the machine gunfire tearing up the woods and roads, in whose gutters, huddled together, lay old men, women and children … Fire enveloped the whole city.

SOURCE 6

Neville Chamberlain, British Prime Minister, 1937 – 1940. He believed that to keep the peace in Europe there was no alternative but to make concessions to Hitler – and many people agreed.

Chamberlain and appeasement

Neville Chamberlain, who became British Prime Minister in 1937, believed that Europe's problems arose from mistakes made at the peace conference in 1919 (see page 7). At that time the Germans had been forced to sign a peace treaty that placed heavy penalties on them. Therefore, although Chamberlain knew Nazi rule was unpleasant, he felt that Hitler's complaints about the Versailles treaty were justified. If these could be satisfied, a lasting settlement might bring peace and stability to the continent.

This policy, known as appeasement (to appease is to pacify), grew out of the genuine desire of many people to avoid the horrors of another war **(Source 7)**. It was believed that there was no defence against the new bombing planes being developed at the time. As one British politician remarked, 'The bomber would always get through' and would be able to reduce cities to rubble.

Appeasement was bound to fail for reasons not clear to everybody at the time. Hitler did not have a horror of war, and his demands went far beyond changing the 1919 peace settlement **(Source 8)**. On 5 November 1937 he outlined his immediate plans at a secret meeting with his generals. He told them that Germany would have to fight Britain and France by 1943 at the latest. If he left it any longer than that, the two countries would have rearmed and, together, would be more powerful than Germany. In the meantime, the Führer intended to create extra 'living space' for Germans, beginning by annexing (taking over) Austria and Czechoslovakia. Some of the generals showed such horror at these dangerous plans that Hitler sacked them.

To achieve his aims, Hitler planned to weaken the governments of Austria and Czechoslovakia from within. In Austria a majority of the population were German and many were Nazi supporters. In Czechoslovakia there were three million Germans cut off from Austria when the

SOURCE 7	
In these notes, dated 26 November 1937, Chamberlain outlines the thinking behind his policy of appeasement.	Both Hitler and Goering said … that they had no desire or intention of making war, and I think we may take this as correct, at any rate for the present. Of course they want to dominate Eastern Europe; they want as close a union with Austria as they can get without incorporating (uniting) her into the Reich (Germany), and they want much the same things for the Sudetendeutsche (Germans in Czechoslovakia) … Now here, it seems to me, is a fair basis for discussion … I don't see why we shouldn't say to Germany, give us satisfactory assurances (promises) that you won't use force to deal with the Austrians and Czechoslovakians, and we will give you similar assurances that we won't use force to prevent the changes you want.

SOURCE 8	
In 1934 Hitler explained his aims to Hermann Rauschnigg, a fellow Nazi.	'We need space', he almost shrieked, 'to make us independent of every possible grouping and alliance. In the east, we must have mastery as far as the Caucasus (mountains in Russia) and Iran. In the west, we need the French coast. We need Flanders (Belgium) and Holland. Above all we need Sweden. We must become a colonial power. We must have a sea power equal to that of Britain … We must rule Europe or fall apart as a nation … Now do you understand why I cannot be limited, either in the east or in the west.'

The Expansion of Nazi Germany, 1936-39

QUESTIONS

1 Why did so many foreigners fight in the Spanish Civil War?

2 What event in Spain in 1937 made people even more afraid of war?

3 Why do you think some of Hitler's generals were horrified by his plans?

4 Why was Hitler's first move against Austria?

SOURCE 9

Hitler enters the capital city of Vienna in triumph during the Nazi annexation of Austria (March 1938).

borders of the new state were drawn up in 1919. They lived in a region known as the Sudetenland. It would not be difficult to play on the grievances of such minorities and use them as an excuse for a Nazi takeover.

Austria was the 'softer' of the two targets. It had a strong Nazi party which had already tried unsuccessfully to seize power in 1934. At that time Italy had been against a move which would have put German troops on its frontier. Consequently Hitler had done little to help the Austrian Nazis. By 1938, however, Hitler's task was easier; Germany and Italy were now allies. Week after week Austrian Nazis, raising the cry '*Anschluss*!' (union with Germany), staged protest marches and riots. Each week Hitler complained publicly that he could not stand by much longer and see these Germans refused their rights.

In March 1938, when it became clear that Italy would not object, the Germans occupied Austria. There was no resistance; in many places cheering crowds greeted the soldiers. Within days Hitler was in Vienna, master of the city where he had nearly starved as a young man **(Source 10)**.

SOURCE 10

On 9 April 1938, when Austria had been taken over by Germany, Hitler said this in a speech in Vienna.

I believe that it was God's will to send a youth from here into the Reich (Germany), to let him grow up, to raise him to be the leader of the nation so as to enable him to lead back his homeland into the Reich … Tomorrow, may every German … bow in humility before the Almighty, who in a few weeks worked such a miracle upon us.

Meeting at Munich

Chamberlain ignored the way the Austrian *Anschluss* had been carried out. Instead, he made excuses for Hitler, pointing out that Austria was really a 'German' country. In fact, it had never been ruled by Germany. And when the Czechs became alarmed because they were now nearly surrounded by German territory, Chamberlain calmed their fears. He reminded them that Hitler had promised, 'I give you my word of honour that Czechoslovakia has nothing to fear from the Reich (Germany)'.

Despite such soothing words, the world soon began to hear from Nazi radio broadcasts about the 'ill-treatment' of Germans in the Sudetenland region of Czechoslovakia. It was true that the Sudeten-Germans were discontented. Until 1919 they had been part of the ruling nationality inside the Austrian empire and they resented having to take orders from a Czech government. Encouraged by Hitler's support, they began to arm themselves for a fight. However, this time events did not run smoothly for the Nazi dictator. The Czechs had a good, well-equipped army, up-to-date armaments factories and a formidable ring of mountain defences. They also had an alliance with France (see page 22). In April 1938 they called up all men of military age and put the armed forces on a war-footing. Both France and Russia promised to come to the Czechs' assistance if Germany attacked.

Hitler was taken aback. In public he still claimed that his intentions towards the Czechs were peaceful. Behind the scenes he told his ministers, 'It is my unalterable decision to smash Czechoslovakia by military action in the near future'. Chamberlain, meanwhile, was alarmed by the Czechs' firm stand. He thought Germany's claim to the Sudetenland was reasonable, arguing that it should never have been part of Czechoslovakia in the first place. With war threatening, he persuaded the French to break their promise to the Czechs and join Britain in urging them to give way to Hitler's demands.

SOURCE 11

The men who signed the Munich agreement on 29 September 1938: (left to right) Chamberlain, Daladier, Hitler, Mussolini and Count Ciano, the Italian Foreign Minister.

When the Czechs still refused to budge, Chamberlain decided to go to Germany and meet Hitler. In all, he had three meetings with Hitler, Mussolini and Daladier, the French Prime Minister. At the last, held in Munich in September, he agreed to let Hitler have the Sudetenland. Soon afterwards German troops occupied this territory. As a result Czechoslovakia lost its mountain defences, much of its railway system, a great deal of valuable industry and large numbers of Czechs who also lived in the Sudetenland. The Czechs felt betrayed by the British, yet so great was the fear of war that Chamberlain returned to England to be treated as a hero **(Source 12)**. He said he brought the hope of 'peace in our time'. Hitler, however, was disappointed. He had wanted the Czechs to defy him so that he would have an excuse to occupy the entire country.

Preparations for war

Europe seemed to have moved back from the brink of war. But Chamberlain's faith in appeasement had been shaken by seeing Hitler at close quarters; he told friends he

thought the Nazi leader was 'half mad'. A massive British rearmament programme was started and some age groups were called up for military service – a thing never done before in peacetime. To counter the threat of bombing, a scheme called ARP – Air Raid Precautions – was begun. Wardens were appointed to patrol the streets, public shelters were dug in parks and many inhabitants of large cities were given metal 'Anderson' shelters to put up in their gardens; these were named after the Home Secretary, Sir John Anderson.

Downing Street, when the Premier reached home last night, was crammed with a crowd that became hysterical. A week before, boos and cries of 'Save the Czechs' had been raised when the Prime Minister returned after his second visit to Hitler. Last evening it was one wild frenzy of cheering. A newspaper seller expressed it in a phrase: 'Public Hero Number One' he shouted … After yells of 'We want Chamberlain', the crowd sang Land of Hope and Glory … You would think, when you heard the cheering, that Britain had really gained a great victory.

Such preparations would not be wasted. Hitler now began to complain for the first time about the ill-treatment of non-Germans; in this case the Slovaks of Czechoslovakia. As Nazi agents set to work to stir up discontent amongst the Slovak population, Nazi radio announced that Slovak leaders had appealed to Hitler for help. Hitler summoned the Czech President to meet him in Berlin to discuss this new 'problem'. At this conference Hermann Goering, commander of the *Luftwaffe* (air force), explained in detail what his bombers could do to Prague, the Czech capital. The President was so frightened that he kept on fainting. Reluctantly, he accepted the occupation of his country.

On 15 March 1939 German units crossed the Czech border, wiping Czechoslovakia from the map 20 years after it had been created at the Paris peace conference. It was the moment of truth for Chamberlain. Hastily, he arranged with the French to guarantee to defend any further country threatened by Nazi Germany.

The Nazi-Soviet pact

Hitler now made a mistake. He decided that Chamberlain and Daladier were cowardly 'little worms' who would never go to war. He felt sure that they would do nothing about his next move which was to be against Poland. Throughout the summer of 1939 Hitler demanded the return of the German port of Danzig (now Gdansk). This had been made a 'free city', open to all nations, in 1919. He also demanded the return of a strip of German territory known as the Polish Corridor. This had been granted to the Poles to give them access to the sea.

The Poles were surprised. They thought they had little to fear from Nazi Germany because they were needed as allies against Russia. They had not objected to the German annexations of Austria and Czechoslovakia, and had even been given a small region of Czechoslovakia. But Hitler wanted Poland as 'living space' for Germans. He reckoned that Britain and France were bluffing when they promised to defend Poland. After all, what could they do to help Poland directly if there were a war? The Nazi leader did not realise that Britain and France had decided that Germany was a threat to their own position in the world. If war came, the two countries would be fighting for themselves, not just Poland.

There remained one problem as far as Hitler was concerned. If war did break out,

QUESTIONS

1 Why would Stalin have been unlikely to ignore a German takeover of Poland?

2 Can you explain why the British Government did not try to stop Hitler by making an alliance with Soviet Russia?

3 Why did the Soviet leaders think Hitler was trying to trick them with the Nazi-Soviet pact (Source 16)?

4 What made the Russians sign the Nazi-Soviet pact?

he had to make sure that Russia did not join in against Germany, making him fight on two fronts. Russia had a keen interest in the fate of Poland which stretched along much of its western border. It was unlikely that Stalin would allow Hitler to take over the country without a fight. In fact, the Soviet dictator tried unsuccessfully to form alliances with Britain and France when he realised Poland was in danger.

Chamberlain did not trust the Soviets, and did not think the Russian army would be much use after the execution of so many of its officers (see page 19). When negotiations between Britain, France and Russia broke down, Hitler saw his chance. He offered the Soviets a treaty of friendship which would give Germany most of Poland but leave Russia with the eastern part of the country. Russia would also be given a free hand to take over Finland and the Baltic states – Estonia, Lithuania and Latvia.

The resulting Nazi-Soviet pact was signed in Moscow on 24 August 1939. It was a strange, dishonest alliance between a Communist leader and a bitter enemy of Communism. Neither dictator trusted the other **(Source 16)**. Stalin calculated that a long war would exhaust Britain, France and

SOURCE 16

Nikita Khrushchev, one of Stalin's officials, describes what happened at a dinner party soon after the Nazi-Soviet Pact was signed.

We knew perfectly well that Hitler was trying to trick us with a treaty. I heard with my own ears how Stalin said, 'Of course, it's all a game to see who can fool whom. I know what Hitler's up to. He thinks he's outsmarted me but actually it's I who have tricked him'. Stalin told Voroshilov (a Soviet general) ... that, because of this treaty, the war would pass us by for a while longer ... We knew that eventually we would be drawn into the war, although, I suppose, Stalin hoped that the English and French might exhaust Hitler and foil his plan to crush the west first and then turn east.

SOURCE 18

The Nazi invasion of Poland began with overwhelming air attacks. Here we see a bewildered Pole standing in the doorway of his ruined home. 'When is the help you promised coming?' he asked a British journalist.

SOURCE 17

Few people forgot what they were doing at the moment war was declared in 1939. Here, a Mr Kynvin described in a radio talk how he felt when the news broke in Britain.

I walked round to the church to see if our wedding was on as arranged. After a satisfactory interview [with the vicar] I started to walk back home. A woman poked her head out of a window and shouted: 'It's war – war – we shall all be bombed to death within a few hours!' ... I was caught without my gasmask (issued in case of a poison gas attack). I rushed into an air raid warden's house and grabbed one, put it on and arrived at our flat fully gasmasked. When Betty saw me, she eventually got hers too, and there we were, waiting for our wedding in about an hour's time, fully gasmasked.

Germany and so benefit Russia. Hitler promised his generals that he would 'crush the Soviet Union' as soon as possible.

The Nazi-Soviet pact made it certain that Hitler would invade Poland. On 1 September 1939 German forces crossed into Poland and occupied Danzig while the *Luftwaffe* devastated Warsaw, the polish capital. The pact also made a wider European war certain. On 3 September Britain and France declared war on Germany **(Source 17)**. Hitler was surprised at the news. 'What do we do now?' he asked those around him. Nobody answered his question, but Goering said, 'If we lose this war, God help us'.

Assessment tasks

A Knowledge and understanding

1 Describe at least three different ways in which the Spanish Civil War proved to be a 'dress rehearsal' for later events in Europe.

2 a What were the long-term factors leading to war in Europe in 1939?
  b What in your opinion were the immediate, or short-term, causes of the war?

3 Explain the following mistaken ideas and attitudes.
  a Why did many British people believe that Hitler's demands could be satisfied short of war? Why were they wrong?
  b Why did the Nazis think Britain and France would not go to war in 1939? Why were they wrong?
  c Why did the Poles think they had little to fear from Nazi Germany? Why were they wrong?

B Interpretations and sources

4 Here are three different views of British policy towards Hitler.

> Neville Chamberlain ... is chiefly remembered for his policy of appeasement of Hitler, a subject which remains highly controversial ... It can be said for this policy, however, that time was gained to unite Britain against Germany by showing that Hitler could only be stopped by war. Thus British entry into the Second World War in September 1939 received almost unanimous support from the country.
> (R.D. Cornwell, 1969)

> In the autumn of 1938 the Luftwaffe had over 1600 bombers in squadron service. France's air force consisted of about 300 fighters and 450 bombers, all of them out of date and practically worthless ... [Britain's] Fighter Command had twenty-nine squadrons (406 planes in all) of which only five were equipped with modern aircraft ... Of the ground defences ... to prevent low-flying attacks on cities, about one-third were ready at the most generous estimate ... Given that information, do you think that Chamberlain had any real alternative but to give in to Hitler at Munich?
> (Tony Howarth, 1979)

> The Munich Agreement ... is usually now seen, as it was by many at the time, including Winston Churchill, as a shameful betrayal by Britain ... [which] lost to the West the valuable Czechoslovak army and the great Skoda munition factories ...[and] handed over nearly a million Czechs to the mercies of Hitler. Much the strongest criticism of Chamberlain's diplomacy, however, lies in his failure to seek support against Hitler from the Soviet Union ... [Against] a solid front of France, Britain, Czechoslovakia and the USSR, Hitler could hardly have succeeded.
> (Denis Richards and Anthony Quick, 1967)

  a Are the differences between these accounts based on fact or opinion, or both? Support your answer with examples.
  b Which account do you find the most convincing, and why?

5 What can we learn from Source 12 about British attitudes towards the Munich Agreement at the time? Include the writer's own views.

6 Look carefully at Source 15.
  a What was the cartoonist's opinion of the Nazi-Soviet pact?
  b Can you explain the words spoken by the two dictators?
  c Whose 'body' lies between them, and why?
  d What other source in this chapter backs up the cartoonist's view of the pact? Which of the two sources is more useful in helping us understand the purpose of the pact? Give reasons for your answer.

Poland to Pearl Harbour 1939–41

In a radio broadcast on Sunday 3 September 1939 Neville Chamberlain announced that Britain was at war with Germany **(Source 1)**. He had hardly finished speaking when a false alarm set air-raid sirens wailing. People rushed to take shelter but there were no attacks. That night searchlight beams swept across empty skies over London and other cities.

SOURCE 1

Here is part of Neville Chamberlain's broadcast.

We have done all that any country could do to establish peace, but a situation in which no word given by Germany's ruler could be trusted, and no people or country could feel itself safe, had become intolerable. Now we have resolved to finish it ... May God bless you all ... It is evil things we shall be fighting against – brute force, bad faith, injustice, oppression and persecution. But against them I am certain that right will prevail.

The 'phoney war'

The expected heavy raids on British towns did not happen because the *Luftwaffe* was busy bombing the Poles. Poland was conquered with surprising speed. The Polish army was large but poorly equipped, with too many cavalry squadrons and insufficient tanks. Aided by good weather, German tank armies, motorised troops and dive-bombers demonstrated the new *Blitzkrieg* (German for 'lightning war'). After ten days the Poles were beaten; charging horsemen, however brave, stood little chance against tanks and aircraft. By 17 September the Germans had crossed western Poland and were approaching lands promised to Stalin in August (see page 33). This forced the Russians to start a hasty invasion of their own. Caught between two powerful enemies, the Poles lost their freedom and independence.

SOURCE 2

A newspaper seller in the Strand, London, announces the outbreak of war (3 September 1939).

Dead horses litter the battlefield after a hopeless fight by Polish cavalry against German tanks and artillery (September 1939).

it found little to do. The French made few attacks, preferring to stay behind the defences of the Maginot Line. The RAF raided Germany, dropping not bombs but leaflets. These urged the German people to overthrow Hitler and make peace. They were used as toilet paper in many homes. At sea, however, there was deadly warfare as Allied fleets tried to prevent German *U-boats* (submarines) sinking British and French shipping.

The only heavy land fighting during the first winter was between Russians and Finns. The Nazi-Soviet Pact had given Russia a free hand to take over the Baltic States: Estonia, Latvia and Lithuania. Stalin established military bases in these countries but when he tried to do the same in Finland, the Finns fought back. In Arctic conditions, they inflicted heavy casualties on the invading Red (Russian) Army until they were finally overwhelmed in March 1940.

This stunning conquest was followed by a period of inactivity during the winter, nicknamed the 'phoney war' by the American press. Although a British Expeditionary Force (BEF) went to France,

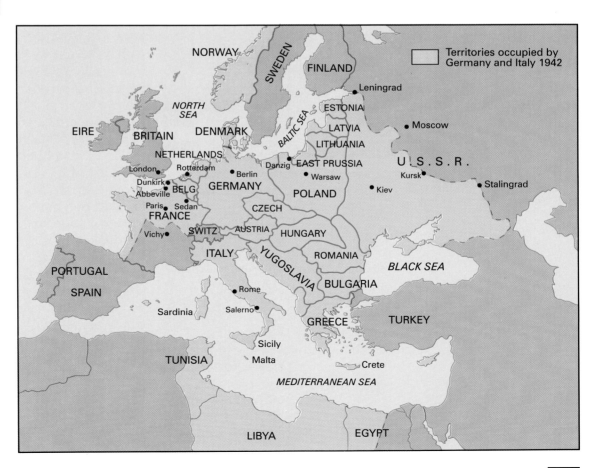

War in Europe, 1939–41

As spring blossomed into early summer a tension entered our lives. Whether we knew it by reason, by overheard conversation, or by instinct, fine weather would bring war. One day Mr. Churchill announced in Parliament that the Royal Navy was laying mines in Norwegian waters – which sounded a rather odd thing to do as Norway was neutral and, so far as we knew, friendly to us. Definitely odd. But not so odd as the news next day that the Germans had landed in Norway.

SOURCE 5

Prime Minister Winston Churchill gives his famous 'V for victory' sign to a group of British sailors.

SOURCE 6

A German general, Walter Nehring, led his troops in an advance which covered 240 miles in 11 days. Here he describes the capture of Abbeville.

Riflemen, artillery and sappers (engineers) took the town in the face of slight resistance and formed a bridgehead across the river. The enemy seemed completely surprised: a British troop were captured on a parade ground, armed only with blanks because they had been carrying out a practice. Nobody had expected the Germans so soon – we hardly expected to arrive so soon ourselves ... At Allonville ... we almost succeeded in capturing an entire squadron of British aircraft ... but they were able to take off at the last minute.

By then Hitler had completed his preparations for war. Two things were uppermost in his mind. Germany has a short coastline so it was easy for British warships to blockade U-boat bases. Also, Germany depended on iron supplies from Sweden for its industries. If Hitler occupied Denmark and Norway, U-boats would have the long Norwegian coastline to operate from and Swedish iron supplies would be secure. The British realised the danger and were considering some sort of action to stop an invasion when Hitler struck first (**Source 4**). In April 1940 German forces overran Denmark and Norway. A British army which landed to assist the Norwegians was driven out.

Miracle at Dunkirk

The British failure in Norway ended Chamberlain's career. He was forced to resign and was replaced by Winston Churchill who took charge of a coalition government of all parties. Churchill had been a soldier, war reporter and writer as well as a politician. He had served as a minister in several governments but became unpopular in the 1930s for his attacks on appeasement. He had urged a tougher line with Hitler and was branded a 'warmonger'. Now the 'warmonger' seemed the best man for the job.

On 10 May 1940 – the day Churchill became Prime Minister – Hitler invaded France, Belgium and Holland. It was the biggest blitz so far. Both Belgians and Dutch were taken by surprise and overwhelmed. Paratroops dropped behind the lines to blow up bridges and railway tracks. Bombers blasted Rotterdam and other Dutch cities. A hundred mile long line of German tanks, armoured cars and lorries broke through the Maginot Line at Sedan after a three-day battle. *Panzer* (armoured) columns raced to the sea at Abbeville (**Source 6**). British troops who had struck north to help the Belgians were cut off. They retreated to Dunkirk, hoping to escape by sea to England.

SOURCE 7

An artist's impression of the Dunkirk evacuation.

The British government appealed to owners of small boats to go to Dunkirk and help rescue the army. Hundreds of 'little ships', including pleasure steamers, yachts, trawlers and motor boats, streamed out of the harbours of southern England to sail into an inferno of death and destruction. For nearly a week, civilians as well as sailors risked their lives to pick up the weary soldiers as they sheltered in sand dunes swept by bullets and bombs (**Sources 8 and 9**). Meanwhile, the Panzers stopped. Perhaps a fierce defence of the town, or the flooded fields outside, held them up. Hitler may have stopped them. He hoped to make peace with Britain; this would not be easy if he had destroyed an entire British army. Whatever the reason for the delay, over 300,000 troops were ferried safely to England by 4 June. It was, Churchill said, 'a miracle of deliverance'.

The fall of France

For the French there was no deliverance. Their enemies were gathering for the kill. Mussolini had not joined Germany in 1939, claiming Italy was not prepared for war. Now, thinking the war was nearly over and anxious to benefit from the peace, he declared war on Britain and France. He seemed to have calculated correctly. On 22 June France surrendered. In the north the Germans took over. In southern France a French government, based at Vichy, was allowed to rule for a time.

SOURCE 8

Private W.B.A. Gaze of the Royal Army Ordnance Corps describes the scene on the beach at Dunkirk on the night of 27 May 1940.

Every ten minutes or so the bombers came over…and we crouched in the little pits we had dug as the bombs came whistling down… Nearly all the bombs fell into the sea… the pall of smoke from the blazing town saved us… Dawn was at hand [and] queues were now waiting in the water… I could see men up to their necks and swimming, fighting for the boats, and naval officers using their revolvers.

SOURCE 9

Charles Lightoller, a retired sailor, took his yacht *Sundowner* to Dunkirk.

At fifty [soldiers on board] I called below, 'How are we getting on?', getting the cheery reply, 'Oh, plenty of room yet'. At seventy-five my son admitted they were getting pretty tight – all equipment and arms being left on deck. I now started to pack them on deck, having passed word below for every man to lie down and keep down … By the time we had fifty on deck, I could feel her (the yacht) getting distinctly tender (unstable), so I took no more. Actually we had 130 on board … Whilst entering [Ramsgate harbour] the men started to get to their feet and she promptly went over at a terrific angle … As [one] officer said, 'God's truth mate! Where did you put them?'. He might well ask.

QUESTIONS

1 Some French people think the British let them down in 1940. What is your view?

2 Why were Hitler and his generals reluctant to invade Britain?

3 Why did the German people think the war had ended with the fall of France?

4 In Source 10, why do you think Churchill makes a point of mentioning the threat to the USA?

The German people thought the war was over. Hitler, however, was eager to attack Russia as soon as possible. He offered Britain peace terms but the British Prime Minister rejected them with contempt. In a series of defiant speeches Churchill inspired the nation, explaining the deadly danger but promising 'Britain will never surrender' **(Source 10)**. Hitler began to prepare Operation Sealion – an invasion of England. His generals and admirals were not enthusiastic; they realised the dangers of a seaborne invasion. But Goering promised an easy victory over the RAF (Royal Air Force) as a first step to gaining control of the Channel. He assured his master that to gain superiority in the air all he needed was 'five days of fine weather'.

Early in August the *Luftwaffe* chief sent his planes against the Hurricane and Spitfire fighters of the RAF. Fierce 'dogfights' raged between British and German aircraft above southern England. People on the ground saw silvery specks wheeling and turning in the clear summer skies. They heard the scream of engines and the harsh rattle of machine guns. Wreckage fell in fields, streets, parks and roads, or sank in the Channel. For the pilots and crew it was strange and alarming. Hours of waiting, perhaps sunbathing in

SOURCE 10

Here is part of a speech Churchill delivered to the House of Commons on 18 June 1940.

The battle of France is over. I expect the battle of Britain is about to begin. Upon this depends the survival of Christian civilisation ... The whole fury and might of the enemy must very soon be turned upon us. Hitler knows that he will have to break us ... or lose the war. If we can stand up to him, all France may be free, and the life of the world may move into broad, sunlit uplands. But if we fail, then the whole world, including the United States, will sink into a new Dark Age.

SOURCE 11

RAF pilots run to their planes during the Battle of Britain.

deckchairs, would be followed by a few dizzy minutes cartwheeling about the sky, earphones alive with shouts, oaths and orders. Some returned safely within a few minutes; others died even more quickly **(Source 12)**.

Slowly the RAF got the upper hand. They were helped by the recent British invention of *radar* (radio detection and ranging) which could be used to detect approaching aircraft over the Channel and so reduce the element of surprise. German bombers proved easy targets once their fighter escorts had been shot down or had returned to base to refuel. On 17 September, when the *Luftwaffe* had lost 1389 planes to the RAF's 790, Hitler postponed the operation indefinitely. In a tribute to the pilots who won the Battle of Britain, Churchill told Parliament, 'Never in the field of human conflict was so much owed by so many to so few'. Battle of Britain pilots have been known as the 'The Few' ever since.

Operation Barbarossa

Mussolini was soon sorry he had gone to war. The Italian navy was crippled by British sea and air strikes. Italian troops were defeated in Africa. His attempts to copy Hitler by annexing Albania and Greece led to bad defeats and the German army had to come to the rescue. In a few short, brutal campaigns Hitler conquered Albania, Greece and Yugoslavia. However, by the summer of 1941 the German leader had completed preparations for his greatest project – Operation Barbarossa (redbeard), an invasion of Russia.

On 22 June 1941 Hitler broke the Nazi-Soviet Pact and sent the German army against Russia. He despised the Red Army after its poor showing in Finland. This war, he told his generals, 'would be like a child's game'. Certainly the Soviet army was poorly equipped and unprepared **(Source 13)**. Stalin was taken by surprise and at first refused to believe the reports. In the first fortnight the Russians lost a million men, nearly all their planes and thousands

SOURCE 12

Pilot Officer John Ellacombe remembers his feelings during the Battle of Britain.

There were fourteen, fifteen hours of daylight each day. You were on duty right through. Chaps were being lost all the time. We had seventeen out of twenty-three killed or wounded ... in less than three weeks. We had another eight aircraft shot down with the chaps unhurt, including myself twice ... There was a tremendous 'twitch'. If somebody slammed a door, half the chaps would jump out of their chairs. There were times when you were so tired, you'd pick up your pint of beer with two hands. But no one was cowering, terrified, in a corner. My greatest fear was that I'd reach the stage where I'd show fear.

SOURCE 13

A Russian general, N.K. Popov, describes the day Operation Barbarossa began.

Army Chief ... Varennikov ... telephoned at 4.30 am and told us that the German artillery was firing along the whole frontier ... that in places they were crossing the frontier ... We all sprang out into the street. It was already light. 'June 22, the longest day' flashed across my mind. The sun was rising – and to meet it came Hitler's heavily loaded bombers ... When they had dropped their bombs, they circled slowly over the town. Why should they hurry? Not one of our fighters was out there; our anti-aircraft guns had not fired a single shot.

SOURCE 14

On 12 October 1941 the German Supreme Army Command issued this order to its troops.

The Führer has reaffirmed his decision that the surrender of Moscow will not be accepted, even if it is offered by the enemy ... Everyone who tries to leave the city and pass through our positions must be fired upon ... For other towns, also, the rule must operate that before they are seized they should be destroyed by artillery fire and air raids, and the population turned to flight. It would be utterly irresponsible ... to feed [Russia's] population at Germany's expense.

of tanks. During August and September German armies drove relentlessly towards Russia's three chief cities – Moscow, the capital, Leningrad (now St. Petersburg) and Kiev. The Nazis took very few prisoners; day after day thousands of men, women and children were killed without mercy **(Source 14)**.

By October, German armies had laid siege to Leningrad and were near Moscow. But brutal Nazi behaviour had united the Russian people even behind a ruler as unpopular as Stalin. Fresh armies were formed from Russia's vast manpower. Entire factories were taken to pieces and moved deep into Asia for safety. As modernised industries began to produce war machines and equipment, the Americans helped with supplies of essential materials. Meanwhile the weather came to the Red Army's aid. Ice and snow slowed the German advance. Their troops had few thick clothes, blankets or warm boots. Guns and rifles iced up. Fires had to be lit under tanks before their engines would start. Men froze to death.

In December, a Russian army equipped with powerful new tanks counter-attacked near Moscow. The German forces were taken by surprise. Hitler at first ordered his men to 'stand and die'. This led to huge casualties. Early in 1942 Hitler allowed them to retreat to special defences, called 'hedgehogs'. Here the Germans lived like starving wolves, holding off an army infuriated by their cruelty.

SOURCE 15

As the German army advanced across Russia, civilians as well as Russian soldiers were shot without mercy. Here we see some Russian survivors trying to identify their dead.

SOURCE 16

President Roosevelt and Prime Minister Churchill at a Sunday church service during their meeting on a British warship (August 1941).

The threat from Japan

From the start of the war it had been clear which side the Americans wanted to win. Their President, Franklin D. Roosevelt, detested Hitler and the Nazis and promised Britain 'all aid short of war'. American factories supplied masses of weapons and equipment to Britain and Russia. American warships often sank U-boats which seemed to threaten their shipping. In August 1941, Roosevelt met Churchill on a British warship off Newfoundland. They signed the Atlantic Charter, which promised 'freedom for all peoples' and a new world peace organisation once Germany was beaten. Yet the American people still argued about whether they should enter a conflict which many said was none of their business **(Source 17)**.

One reason for this American reluctance was the threat from Japan. Since the invasion of Manchuria in 1931 (see page 23) the Japanese had continued their policy of seizing new territory to provide raw materials and extra living space for their people. In 1937 they attempted to conquer China. It was the start of a long and savage war in that country. In 1940, when France fell, the Japanese occupied French Indo-China (now Vietnam). Only fear of an attack by Russia, whose armies stood on the Manchurian border, kept them in check.

Hitler's invasion of Russia removed this danger to Japan. With the Red Army fully

SOURCE 17

In June 1940, as Americans argued about whether to go to war, the editor of one newspaper contemplated a Nazi victory in Europe.

If we do not help the Allies (Britain and France), if we turn our backs on them, they will see no reason for helping us by giving us their fleets ... If these fleets go to Hitler, he will have power to take British possessions in the West Indies. These islands control the Panama Canal (administered by the USA) ... He will not move [against the USA] without the British or French fleets. But he will move in then, and war will be certain.

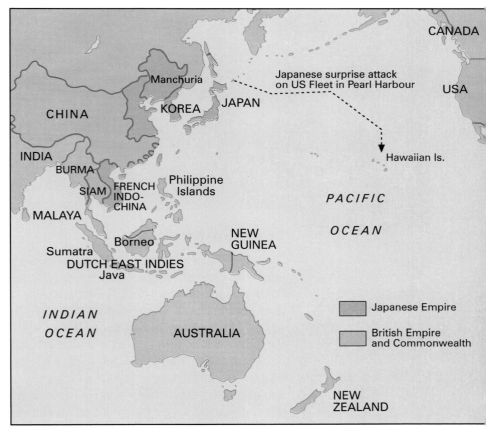

The Far East at the time of Pearl Harbour (1941)

occupied, Japan's war chiefs could plan widespread conquests in the Far East. Roosevelt was concerned about the safety of American territories in the Pacific such as the Philippines and Hawaii. To try to prevent further Japanese expansion, he stopped exports of oil to Japan. This was a serious blow to a country with no oil of its own. The Japanese Emperor, Hirohito, was informed by his advisers that Japan was 'like a fish in a pond from which the water is gradually being drained away'.

Pearl Harbour

The American oil ban left Japan's leaders with two choices. Either they must give up their conquests, as the US demanded, or they could seize a number of oil-rich islands in the Dutch East Indies (now Indonesia). By November 1941, when discussions between Japan and the USA finally broke down, it was clear that the Japanese government had chosen war. American spies reported large Japanese naval forces heading towards the East Indies and the British colony of Malaya. Rumours that a third fleet, with aircraft carriers, was on its way to Hawaii were not taken seriously. Consequently it came as a complete surprise when hundreds of Japanese aircraft appeared over the US naval base at Pearl Harbour in Hawaii just after dawn on 7 December 1941.

It was a peaceful Sunday morning. Along the seashore lights still flickered outside a few night clubs and radios blared out dance music. In the harbour the line of US battleships, anchored in pairs, offered a perfect target. The Japanese attack had been planned carefully, even taking into account favourable tides. Some planes carried bombs, others torpedoes. The result was devastating destruction (**Source 19**).

This is part of President Roosevelt's speech to the US Congress the day after Pearl Harbour.

Yesterday, December 7 1941 – a date which will live in infamy (shame or disgrace) – the United States of America was suddenly and deliberately attacked by ... the Empire of Japan. The United States was at peace with that nation and ... was still in conversation with its government ... Indeed, one hour after the Japanese air squadrons ... commenced bombing ... the Japanese ambassador ... delivered a formal reply to a recent American message ... This reply ... contained no threat or hint of war ... [yet] the distance of Hawaii from Japan makes it obvious that the attack was planned many days or weeks ago.

The battleship *Arizona* blew up and sank in a mass of burning oil, taking a thousand men down with her. The destroyer *Shaw* was demolished in a huge mushroom of fire and smoke. Only four US fighter planes managed to get airborne; 117 were destroyed on the ground. By midday, eight battleships had been sunk or disabled and 2403 men killed.

Two US aircraft carriers were away from Hawaii on patrol that morning. They returned to find wrecked and sunken ships, oil-covered water, smoking ruins and floating bodies. A furious President Roosevelt declared war on Japan the next day **(Source 21)**. Hitler considered the dramatic turn of events for a few days, then decided the time was ripe to punish the Americans for helping his enemies. He had a treaty of friendship with Japan and was certain that the war with Russia was nearly won. On 11 December he declared war on the United States. It was his greatest mistake and it led to world war.

SOURCE 20

The Japanese attack on Pearl Harbour: a dense cloud of smoke hangs over the US warships *West Virginia* and *Tennessee*

Assessment tasks

A Knowledge and understanding

1 What were the consequences for Britain of Hitler's decision to invade Russia in June 1941? Distinguish between immediate consequences and longer term ones.

2 How did the following affect the course of the war?

   a Germany's need to import iron.
   b Japan's need to import all its oil.

3 In which country or countries involved in the war,

   a were the Nazis hated and feared?
   b was Germany considered a friend or ally?
   c might the people have welcomed the German army if it had treated them better?

Give reasons for each answer.

B Interpretations and sources

4 Here two historians try to explain Hitler's decision to declare war on the USA.

> Hitherto Hitler had shown considerable patience in face of growing aid given by the US government to the British. But he was coming to the conclusion that a virtual state of war already existed with the USA, and there was no point in delaying the clash... Two other factors affected Hitler's decision. The first was his disastrous underestimate of American strength ... The second ... [was that] the prospect of a war embracing the whole world excited Hitler's imagination.
> (Alan Bullock, 1952)

> Hitler's contempt for the Americans, coupled with his personal dislike of Roosevelt, was one of the strongest influences on his decision to declare war ... He was convinced that the Americans were going to declare war on Germany anyway and he wanted to avoid them 'stealing a march on us' ... Hitler remained confident ... that ... he would smash the Russians quickly before American help could become effective. In such circumstances the USA would be reluctant to become involved in a land war in Europe.
> (N. Henderson, 1993)

   a How are these accounts similar and how are they different?
   b What sort of evidence seems to be lacking?
   c Which account do you find the most convincing, and why?

5 a How do Sources 6 and 13 help to explain the success of the attacks they describe?
   b Compare these sources with Source 19.

6 Sources 8 and 11 were written by men who bravely risked their lives. Which is the more useful in helping us understand how it felt to be in this situation? Give reasons for your answer.

5 The Defeat of Nazi Germany

War in Europe and North Africa, 1941–45

On 12 June 1941 Rudolf Rossler, a German journalist living in Switzerland, picked up a radio message from officers at German Army Headquarters. Both Rossler and his secret informants were enemies of Nazism and wanted Hitler to lose the war. The message revealed the date for the start of Operation Barbarossa – 22 June. Rossler passed on the information but Stalin refused to believe it. After it proved correct the Soviet dictator recruited Rossler to spy for Russia, using the codename Lucy. During 1943 the Lucy Spy Ring – Rossler and the officers – were to play a vital role.

Stalingrad and Kursk

After their setback near Moscow (see page 42) in 1942 the Germans drove south to the Russian oilfields and city of Stalingrad (now called Volgograd). They made good progress and, by August, were smashing their way into the suburbs of Stalingrad. From his hide-out in the ruins, a Red Army soldier saw 'drunken Nazis jumping off trucks, playing mouth organs and dancing on the pavements'.

These men were celebrating too soon. Once inside the wilderness of rubble and ruins, their tanks, lorries and armoured cars were of little use. The battle became a man-to-man struggle at close quarters. During daylight hours the Germans held their own because they were better armed and could call on aircraft for help. At night it was a

SOURCE 2

A Russian soldier in Stalingrad describes what happened after the Germans captured his comrade, Berdyshev.

What Berdyshev told the Germans I don't know ... He had led them up the garden path (tricked them) because an hour later they started to attack at precisely that point where I had put my machine gun ... They came out impudently, standing up and shouting. They came down the street in a column ... I sent a belt (250 bullets) into the yelling, dirty-grey Nazi mob. I was wounded in the hand but I did not let go of the machine gun. Heaps of bodies littered the ground ... An hour later the Germans led Berdyshev on to a heap of ruins and shot him ... for having shown the way to my machine gun.

different story. Russians fell upon them in the dark, killing with bayonet, knife or bare hands. For two months this dreadful battle raged from street to street, house to house, cellar to cellar **(Source 2)**.

In November 1942 fresh Russian armies started to encircle the city. The German commander wanted to get out before it was too late. Goering promised Hitler he could supply the army by air so the German commander's request was refused. In fact, winter snowstorms and fog soon stopped all flights. The Germans ran out of fuel, ammunition and food. A well trained army became a starving rabble, wrapped in rags and gnawing horsemeat. Three hundred thousand men had entered Stalingrad in August. Only 90,000 were alive to surrender in February 1943. Of these, less than 6000 ever saw Germany again.

In spite of this shattering defeat, Germany was still a formidable power, with ten million fighting men backed by all the resources of Nazi-dominated Europe. In June 1943 the German army went on the offensive again, hoping to destroy a huge Russian force grouped around the town of Kursk. As their generals made final plans,

SOURCE 3

Russian troops in the ruins of Stalingrad. The Red Army kept enough forces in the city to pin down the Germans while preparing to encircle them.

the Lucy Spy Ring supplied information to the Russians. Every detail was revealed, including the location of supply depots, airstrips and gun positions, the number and strength of units and their weapons, equipment and lines of advance. British Intelligence also supplied information after breaking the secret code used by the German military command. Consequently, before the German attack the Red Army let loose a hurricane of artillery fire on carefully selected targets.

The Germans realised they had been betrayed but it was too late to change the plan. In the Battle of Kursk, the biggest tank battle of the war, they were utterly defeated, losing 500,000 men killed, wounded or captured **(Source 5)**. After this, Hitler knew he could not beat Russia. 'The God of War has gone over to the other side', he remarked gloomily.

SOURCE 5

During the battle of Kursk, Otto Richter, a German soldier, wrote this to his brother. Richter was killed before he could post it.

Dear Kurchen,
You know me, I have never been one for losing my head or panicking. I have always believed firmly in our aims and in victory. But now I want to say goodbye to you. Don't be surprised. I really mean goodbye and forever. We attacked not long ago. If only you knew how disgusting and horrible it was. Our soldiers went forward bravely but the Russian devils wouldn't go back for anything, and every metre cost us the lives of our comrades ... There aren't many of us left ... only 18 in our company ... God, how will it all end? ... What's the point of living if the war's lost?

Alamein and Italy

In November 1941 British forces overran the Italian North African colony of Libya. Once again the Germans had to come to the Italians' rescue. The *Afrika Korps* – troops specially trained in desert warfare – landed in Africa and advanced along the coast to threaten Egypt, a British possession. The German commander, Erwin Rommel, knew that a conquest of Egypt would give Germany control of the Suez Canal – a vital link between Britain and its territories in the Far East. It would also allow the Germans to seize the rich oilfields of the Middle East.

At first Rommel was successful, driving the British 8th Army out of Libya. But in June 1942 he was halted in a fierce battle

SOURCE 6

Erwin Rommel, commander of Hitler's *Afrika Korps,* had been one of the successful generals in the invasion of France. He was nicknamed 'the Desert Fox'.

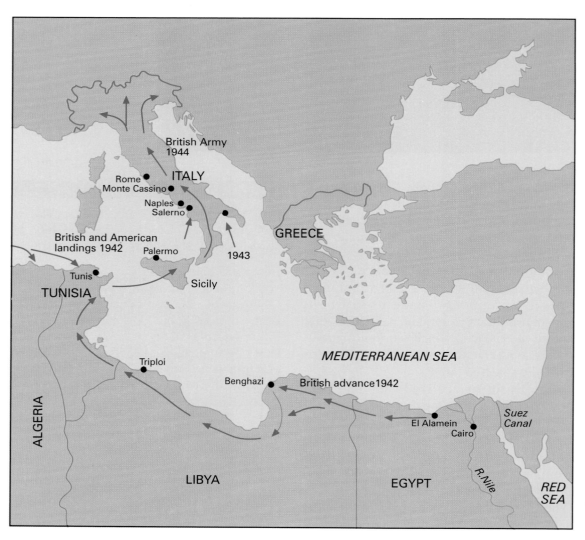

War in North Africa and Italy.

General Montgomery had an unusual way of addressing his troops. Here George Greenfield, an officer at El Alamein, describes his feelings on the night before the battle.

The full moon was very bright on October 23 as we moved up to our start-line ... I picked up a piece of paper ... It was one of the printed broadsheets that the Army Commander had had distributed ... General Montgomery was no stranger to our battalion ... We had served under him for a year [in England] ... We had not loved him then and on this particular night our affection had, if anything, diminished ... [It] did not strike us as an occasion for cricketing slogans like 'hit the enemy for six out of Africa'. It was not hard to sit in the pavilion of Army Headquarters and urge others to face the fast bowling.

QUESTIONS

1 Why did the war spread to the deserts of North Africa?

2 The battles of Stalingrad and El Alamein are generally regarded as turning points in the war. Can you explain why?

3 Can you think of reasons why the western Allies began their counter-offensive in Italy?

4 What were the advantages, from the Allies' point of view, of trying to bomb Germany into surrender?

only 60 miles from the Egyptian city of Cairo. Although it was a British success, it did not satisfy Churchill who sacked the 8th Army Commander, General Auchinleck, and appointed Bernard Montgomery in his place. Aided by massive reinforcements of men and equipment, and against an *Afrika Korps* starved of fuel by air attacks, Montgomery won a decisive victory at El Alamein in October **(Source 7)**. The remains of Rommel's army retreated across Libya into Tunisia, only to be trapped by British and American forces led by the US General Eisenhower. In May 1943 over 250,000 German and Italian soldiers were captured, although Rommel himself escaped to Germany. Africa had been cleared of the enemy. The Allies could now concentrate on freeing Europe from the grip of the Nazi dictator.

In July 1943 British and American forces crossed the Mediterranean, guarded by warships and planes. They occupied the island of Sicily after a heavy bombardment and made landings in Italy. Their arrival on Italian soil led to the fall of Mussolini, who was rescued from his enemies by German paratroopers and taken north. When the new Italian government made peace with the Allies the Germans invaded Italy. For the next two years clever German defence of a succession of river and mountain positions slowed the Allied advance. A landing at Salerno, near Naples, was nearly driven back into the sea. At Monte Cassino it took four months to drive the Germans from the hills around an ancient monastery. It was June 1944 before Rome was captured and April 1945 before the final victory in Italy.

Bombers and U-boats

After the fall of France, in 1940, Britain's only means of hitting at Germany was by air attack. This pleased some RAF commanders who were convinced that the Germans could be beaten by bombing alone. They claimed that once German industries were crippled and the people terrorised, Hitler would be forced to surrender. By 1942 the RAF had long-range Halifax, Stirling and Lancaster bombers suitable for the task. The US Air Force, which had bases in Britain from 1942, was equipped with heavily armed Boeing 'Flying Fortresses'. Such aircraft could reach most German cities to drop high explosive and fire-bombs. The air chiefs were very keen on fire as a weapon. While the effects of explosions were limited, they were sure that fires, once started in sufficient numbers, would spread and destroy an entire city.

In 1942 Air Chief Marshal Arthur Harris took over RAF Bomber Command. No man believed more firmly in bombing as a war-winner; he once refused to allow aircraft to

be used to drop paratroopers because he said men did not explode! On 30 May Harris launched the first 'thousand-bomber' night raid on the German city of Cologne. By morning much of the city had been devastated and thousands of people killed. A column of smoke 5000 metres high rose above the ruins **(Source 9)**. Altogether, about 650,000 German civilians died in raids of this kind, many as a result of terrifying 'firestorms'. Even so, the Allied bombers never succeeded in crippling German industry or crushing the spirit of the people.

SOURCE 9

A *Daily Mail* reporter describes the bombing of Cologne on 30 May 1942.

Our bombers arrived over Cologne ... from all over England. Very soon the city was a great beacon – visible 140 miles away – to guide the incoming bombers all the way from the Dutch coast. In the words of one Halifax pilot, 'It was almost too gigantic to be real ... Below us every part of the city buildings were ablaze. Here and there you could see their outlines, but mostly it was just one big stretch of fire. It looked at times as if we were on fire ourselves, with a red glow dancing up and down the wings.

Throughout the war it was vital for Britain to keep open her sea routes in the face of heavy German attacks. In peacetime, over half of all British goods, including food and raw materials, were imported. If this 'lifeblood' were cut off Britain's industry would collapse and its people run short of food. Moreover, from 1942 American armies and their equipment had to be brought across the Atlantic. The Germans' main weapons in this 'Battle of the Atlantic' were the long-range bomber and the U-boat. Germany's surface fleet was not large enough to take on the might of the British navy.

In 1940 the German navy took over bases along the French and Belgian coasts which gave U-boats easy access to the Atlantic. During the next three years British and Allied merchant shipping suffered terrible losses, including the deaths of 30,000 seamen. The tide did not begin to turn until the spring of 1943, as U-boats were hunted with increasing success by long-range aircraft using searchlights and radar. By 1944 German submarine 'wolfpacks' were virtually driven off the main Atlantic sea routes.

SOURCE 10

Another U-boat victim sinks in the Atlantic (1942). This photograph was taken from the U-boat that fired the torpedo.

SOURCE 11

The 'big three' - (from left to right) Stalin, Roosevelt and Churchill - at their meeting in Teheran in 1943. At these talks Stalin insisted that Russia must have a say in the government of Poland after the war.

SOURCE 12

This comes from the diaries of Lord Moran, Churchill's doctor, who was at the Teheran conference.

Before long the session developed into a wrangle (argument) between the PM (Churchill) and Stalin. Stalin said he could see no point in the British fighting their way up Italy, foot by foot ... The PM said they were all agreed that the invasion of France must come first, but we were short of landing craft and there might be delays ... As far as I can make out the President (Roosevelt) supported Stalin ... Stalin said ... 'Russia is only interested in Overlord (codename for an invasion of France)'... He demanded that a date be fixed and we all keep to it.

D-Day

The Allied leaders, Churchill, Roosevelt and Stalin, met for the first time at Teheran, in Iran, in November 1943. Stalin accused Roosevelt and Churchill of delaying an invasion of western Europe in order to weaken Russia in its struggle with Germany. He demanded that a 'second front' against Germany be opened up in France as soon as possible **(Source 12)**.

Churchill had fought in France during the First World War and realised the slaughter which might follow an Allied landing. He did not oppose Stalin's request but suggested that new fronts should be opened up in Greece and Turkey. Behind Churchill's proposals was the hope that British and American troops could get into eastern Europe before the Red Army arrived and imposed Communist rule. Roosevelt seemed unconcerned about this danger. The US President was anxious that Russia should join in the war against Japan once Germany was defeated. Churchill was soon forced to drop his east European schemes in favour of an invasion of France.

On 'D' (for deliverance) Day – 6 June 1944 – a fleet of 5000 ships landed British, American, French and Canadian troops on the Normandy coast. The supreme commander of 'Operation Overlord' was Eisenhower, with Montgomery in direct charge of military matters. The choice of Normandy for the landings surprised the Germans. They had expected the assaults to come further north, possibly around Calais. The men stormed selected beaches, codenamed Sword, Juno, Utah, Omaha and Gold **(Source 14)**.

Some landings found the Germans unprepared. Utah beach was taken for the loss of only twelve men. At Gold it was so quiet that one British soldier asked, 'Is this a private beach?' But at Omaha things went badly wrong for the Americans. Stranded on an open beach by variable tides, they were

SOURCE 13

Generals Eisenhower (left) and Montgomery inspect troops in England during the build-up to D-Day. Two years of planning and preparation were necessary before the Allied invasion could be launched.

QUESTIONS

1. Why was the Atlantic Ocean such an important battleground for most of the war?

2. In what way were the Allied leaders not completely honest with each other when they met at Teheran in 1943?

3. Looking at the map on page 55, can you explain why the Germans expected the Allied landings to be near Calais?

4. Why do you think the German army fighting in Normandy in 1944 included many teenagers?

SOURCE 14

Charles Wilson, a British soldier, went ashore on D-Day.

We hit two mines going in – bottle mines on stakes. They didn't stop us, although our ramp was damaged and an officer standing on it was killed. We grounded on a sandbank. The first man off was a commando sergeant in full kit. He disappeared like a stone into six feet of water ... The beach was strewn with wreckage, a blazing tank, bundles of blanket and kit, bodies and bits of bodies. One bloke near me was blown in half by a shell and his lower part collapsed in a bloody heap in the sand.

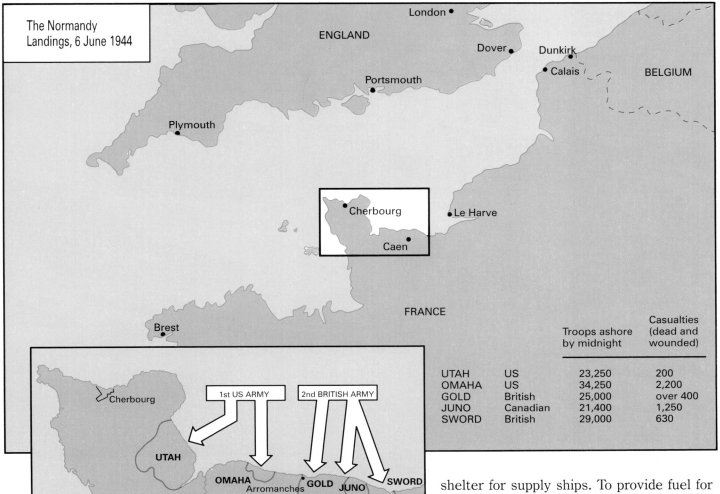

The Normandy Landings, 6 June 1944

		Troops ashore by midnight	Casualties (dead and wounded)
UTAH	US	23,250	200
OMAHA	US	34,250	2,200
GOLD	British	25,000	over 400
JUNO	Canadian	21,400	1,250
SWORD	British	29,000	630

1st US ARMY

2nd BRITISH ARMY

— Limits of Allied advance after 24 hours

slaughtered by Germans entrenched in high cliffs. An American sailor off-shore reported, 'The beach is littered with burning vehicles and dead and dying troops'. It took hours for small groups of survivors to inch their way inland. Using rocks and holes as shelter, they drove the Germans from their defences in hand-to-hand fighting.

Two new inventions featured in the Normandy landings. The Allies realised it was unlikely that a large French port would be captured quickly, so temporary harbours, called 'mulberries', were built in England and towed across the Channel to provide shelter for supply ships. To provide fuel for the armies, a pipeline called PLUTO (Pipeline Under the Ocean) was laid on the seabed from England to France. It came into use six weeks after D-Day but broke soon afterwards. By that time a large army was firmly established ashore (**Source 16**) and the port of Cherbourg had been captured.

The Germans continued to fight with great skill and courage. But they had no hope of victory now that Germany was under attack from both east and west. One German general told the High Command, 'Make peace, you fools! What else is there to do?'

The advance on Berlin

Hitler, of course, knew the Allies would never make peace with him. He could expect little mercy from Stalin, and Roosevelt had demanded that Germany

US troops get their vehicles and equipment ashore on D-day. Notice the barrage balloons in the sky, put up to stop enemy aircraft flying low.

Mary Mulrey was an army nurse working in a hospital at Bayeux in Normandy during the battle. This is an extract from her diary.

5 July 1944. We had a convoy of young Canadian casualties brought in this morning ... There were stretchers all down the middle of the tent; there were charred bodies everywhere, some were quiet and dying, others screaming with pain, all with severe burns. We moved the dead out of the ward and got on trying to save the living. They were all so young and frightened ... A young officer told me what had happened ... The Canadians wear a darker shade of khaki uniform [than the British] ... similar to the Germans. Our troops attacked them with flamethrowers, thinking they were the enemy.

surrender 'unconditionally'. In refusing to admit defeat, Hitler listened less and less to advice and did his best to shut out all unpleasant news. In July 1944 some German officers tried to kill Hitler and make peace before Germany was overrun. They placed a bomb near him at a conference but he escaped almost unhurt when it exploded. A false report that he was dead brought the conspirators into the open. When they discovered what had happened, some killed themselves to avoid capture. Others were not so lucky. They were arrested, tortured, tried and hanged with piano wire.

Desperate German resistance by an army now containing many fanatical Nazi teenagers pinned down Allied troops in Normandy far longer than they had expected. It was August before the Germans were defeated and Paris captured. In September, Montgomery made a bold

SOURCE 17

A painting of the Rhine bridge at Arnhem during the battle in 1944. When lightly-armed British paratroopers landed they were surprised to find two German tank divisions in the town.

attempt to cross the river Rhine – the main obstacle barring the way into Germany. Paratroopers were dropped in Holland to seize several Rhine bridges and hold them until the main army broke through. The plan failed because the tanks could not reach the most northerly bridge, at Arnhem, in time. After a heroic fight most of the paratroopers in the town were killed or captured. The angry Germans took a grim revenge on the population. Dutch civilians who had helped Allied soldiers were shot or imprisoned. During the 'hunger winter' that followed the battle, food supplies ran short and 18,000 people starved to death **(Source 18)**.

Soon after D-Day the Russians attacked in the east, driving the Germans back on all fronts. In Poland they wiped out half the German forces facing them. This success

SOURCE 18

Ben De Vries lived through the 'hunger winter' in Holland. He describes life at the time.

We had neither heat nor light in the winter of 1944. No gas, electricity, not even candles. We'd use tiny generators on bicycles and each person would pedal away for a few minutes ... I lost so much weight; I was down to 39 kilograms ... In January 1945 we went ... to farmers in Friesland (a province of Holland) where food was plentiful ... As barter (exchange) for food I'd taken along silver cutlery ... we'd received on our engagement ... I arrived home with bacon, cheese, suet, skim-milk and potatoes. All more valuable than silver and gold.

encouraged the people of Warsaw, the Polish capital, to rise in revolt against Nazi rule. But the Russians were either unwilling or unable to arrive in time to help. After 63 days of savage fighting, the Poles were massacred by 'death squads' of criminals from local prisons. The city was deliberately destroyed. In the meantime the Russians invaded the German province of East Prussia. Its people were given a taste of what the Russians had suffered when the Germans invaded them. The town of Konigsberg contained 42,000 bodies and a few shell-shocked civilians when it was captured.

Further south, the Red Army cleared Romania, Hungary and Yugoslavia of Germans. Some of the inhabitants welcomed the Russian troops as 'liberators'. In Yugoslavia the Russians were helped by local Communists who had been fighting the Germans for years. But the Hungarians had been Hitler's allies. They fought fiercely to defend their capital, Budapest. Yet nothing could stop the Russian advance. In late March they laid siege to Berlin, a ruined city where the citizens were described as 'half mad ... starving, clawing their way into battered food shops ... slinking for shelter in cellars'.

Below the Chancellery (German government building) in the capital Hitler lived a weird existence, issuing instructions which showed he was out of touch with reality. Towns which had fallen were told to fight to the last. Dead generals were appointed to command armies which no longer existed. Meanwhile, his enemies drew nearer every day. In March the Rhine was at last crossed by Americans who found an undamaged bridge at Remagen. Later, the British got over in gliders and assault boats. By mid-April 1945 Vienna, capital of Austria, had fallen to the Allies. On the 25th American and Russian troops met for the first time, near Berlin. On the 28th Hitler heard that Mussolini had been captured and shot by Italian Communists. Two days later he killed himself **(Source 20)**. The war lasted another week. On 7 May 1945 Germany surrendered unconditionally.

SOURCE 19

A Red Army officer hoists the Soviet flag on a building in Berlin. This comes from a Russian film made to celebrate victory over Nazi Germany.

SOURCE 20

Otto Gunsche was Hitler's valet (personal servant). Here he describes his master's last moments on 30 April 1945. Eva Braun was Hitler's girlfriend whom he had married a few hours before.

When the door of the Führer's apartment closed, there was a moment's silence ... I stood by the door like a sentry ... After hearing the shot, I went into the room ... Hitler's body was crumpled up, his head hanging towards the floor. Blood was running from his right temple on to the carpet. The pistol had fallen to the ground. Eva was sitting on the other corner of the sofa, her legs curled under her (she had taken poison) ... Later the two bodies were placed in a trench ... and doused with petrol. We managed to light the fire by throwing pieces of flaming paper into the trench ... As the flames shot up all the men ... raised their arms in the Nazi salute.

Assessment tasks

A Knowledge and understanding

1 'We have only to kick at the front door and the whole rotten Russian building will come tumbling down.' (Hitler, 1941)
   a Why was Hitler so confident of a quick victory over Russia?
   b Why was he proved wrong? In your answer distinguish between (i) military reasons and (ii) other reasons.

2 In what ways did the British, Americans and Russians have different war aims in Europe? Give reasons for the differences.

3 Rank in order of importance the following factors in the eventual defeat of Nazi Germany. Give reasons for your answer.
   ● The war in the air
   ● The war at sea
   ● The land war in western Europe
   ● The land war in eastern Europe
   ● The land war in North Africa and southern Europe

B Interpretations and sources

4 On 13-14 February 1945 the German city of Dresden, defenceless and crowded with refugees, was destroyed by nearly 3000 British and American bombers. Writers have argued ever since about the rights and wrongs of such an attack.

   The main reason for the attack on Dresden ... which almost certainly killed at least 60,000 people ... seems to have been that the Commander-in-Chief of Bomber Command, Sir Arthur Harris ... believed that bombing could and would by itself somehow destroy the enemy's ... will to continue the war.
   (Mark Arnold Forster, 1973)

   Nobody has admitted responsibility for ordering the Dresden raid, but it now seems clear that it originated at a level higher than [Bomber] Command itself. It may well have been a ... gesture to impress the advancing Russians (who occupied the city soon after) with Western airpower. Civilian death figures ... would have been higher had not some bomber crews ... deliberately pitched their loads wide.
   (Gavin Lyall, 1968)

   The attack on Dresden was no different in character from previous attacks on other towns ... Ministers had never been ... frank with the public ... They had always pretended that the bomber offensive was being conducted against strategic targets and that German civilians were being killed only by a regrettable accident.
   (A.J.P. Taylor, 1965)

   The memorial fountains in Dresden, proudly erected to commemorate successful aggression [against France] in 1870 ... [were] choked with German corpses, thanks to Bomber Command, in 1945 ... Is it not possible that ... one lasting benefit resulted ... namely that it brought home to the Germans as nothing else could have done the real meaning of the war they had started?
   (Norman Longmate, 1983)

   a In what ways do these accounts differ? Do the differences concern matters of fact, opinion or both?
   b Which of the viewpoints expressed here do you find convincing, and why?

5 What do Sources 5 and 7 tell you about the differing attitudes of soldiers towards the war?

6 Compare the usefulness of Sources 9 and 18 as descriptions of the sufferings of civilians. One is more informative than the other. Can you give a reason why?

6 The Defeat of Japan

War in Asia, 1941–45

SOURCE 1

Hiroshima after the atomic bomb exploded on 6 August 1945. Five square miles of Japan's eighth largest city were reduced to radioactive ashes. *Inset*: The B29 Super-Fortress which dropped the bomb returns from its mission.

On 6 August 1945 an American aircraft dropped an atomic bomb on the Japanese city of Hiroshima, killing at least 80,000 people and turning it into a wasteland. Midori Naka, a famous actress, was making breakfast when a blinding light filled the kitchen. 'My first thought was that the hot water boiler must have exploded', she recalled. With the house collapsing around her, she struggled from the wreckage. Outside the street was on fire. She joined the panic-stricken thousands who were running towards the river to escape the heat (**Source 2**) and threw herself in. She might have drowned like many others but soldiers fished her out.

Midori was put on one of the few trains to leave the city that day and taken to hospital in Tokyo, the Japanese capital. Here she was attended by specialists who wanted to find out more about the 'mystery illness' which had broken out among survivors at Hiroshima. At first, the actress seemed shaken but unhurt by her experiences. Then her beauty began to fade. Her hair fell out, her face became wrinkled and purple patches 'as big as

Mrs Futaba Kitayama was just a mile from the centre of the blast at Hiroshima. Here she describes the experience.

An enemy plane appeared all alone, very high ... Its silver wings shone brightly in the sun ... At that moment a shattering flash filled the sky ... I was thrown to the ground ... debris kept falling, beams and tiles piled on top of me ... Finally, I did manage to crawl free ... I rubbed my nose and mouth with a towel ... To my horror I found that the skin of my face had come off on the towel ... The skin of my left hand fell off too; the five fingers, like a glove ... People ... were running to the river ... their faces were puffy and ashen, their hair tangled, they held their hands raised ... groaning with pain ... On a parade ground ... a number of secondary school children ... were writhing in agony ... crying 'Mama'!

pigeons' eggs' covered her body. When she died on 24 August the doctors knew she was a victim of radiation poisoning caused by the bomb. Some radiation victims survived for years. In 1962 a Japanese doctor was asked, 'When was your last bomb death?' 'Yesterday', he replied.

Ten days before Midori's death Japan had surrendered after a second atomic bomb devastated the city of Nagasaki.

Japan's new empire

Few Japanese could have foreseen such a terrible end to the war. After the lightning strike on Pearl Harbour, Japan won a series of spectacular victories. The Philippine Islands, ruled by the United States, were captured after fierce fighting. The Dutch East Indies (now Indonesia) were seized

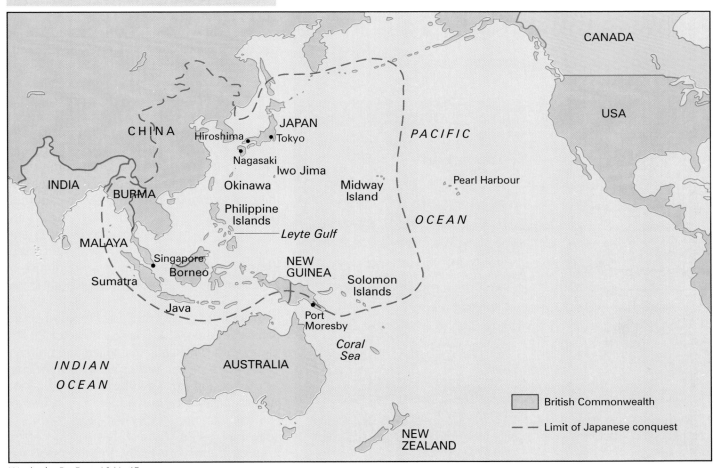

War in the Far East, 1941–45

British and Indian troops driven out of Burma by the Japanese reached India in May 1942, after a 1000-mile retreat. Their commander, General Slim, describes their condition.

Ploughing their way up slopes, over a track inches deep in slippery mud, soaked to the skin, rotten with fever, ill-fed and shivering as the air grew colder, the troops went on, hour after hour, day after day. Their only rest at night was to lie on the sodden ground under the dripping trees, without even a blanket to cover them up ... All of them, British, Indian and Gurkha, were gaunt and ragged as scarecrows ... Yet ... they still carried their arms and kept their ranks ... they were still recognisable as fighting units.

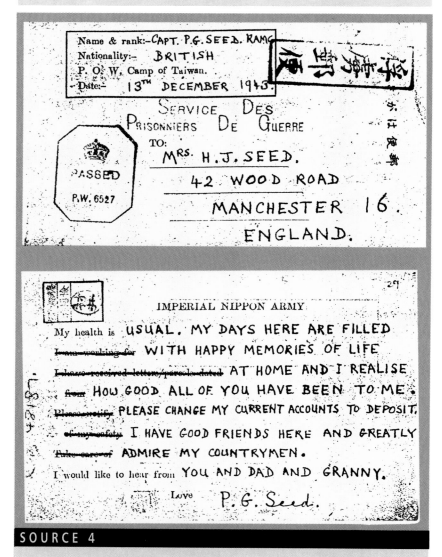

The Japanese rarely allowed prisoners of war to write home. Captain P.G. Seed was held on the island of Taiwan when he wrote this to his mother – on a postcard supplied by his captors.

and Malaya, Hong Kong, Singapore and Burma taken from the British **(Source 3)**. By the summer of 1942 Japan controlled all the world's rubber, 70 per cent of its tin and plentiful supplies of oil. For a nation with few raw materials of its own these were rich prizes.

Against Japan's experienced soldiers the Dutch, British and American troops were badly equipped and often poorly trained. Against the Japanese navy of 200 warships the Allies in the Far East had only 90; against 7500 planes they had only 1000. Allied possessions were spread across thousands of miles of ocean. The Japanese could concentrate their forces and attack where they wished. Even so, there was no time to lose from the Japanese point of view. The United States was a far greater industrial and military power than Japan. The new Japanese empire must be developed before the Americans had time to recover from the first shock. It was a gamble, but with the USA fighting Germany as well, it was a gamble that might succeed.

Japan's conquests meant that for the first time an Asian power had taken possessions from the proud Westerners, often with astonishing ease. It was a great chance for Japan to become the champion and protector of Asia against its old European and American masters. Unfortunately it soon became clear that colonial peoples had merely exchanged one master for another. The Japanese ruled with an iron hand, ruthlessly exploiting local resources and savagely punishing anybody who protested. Before long 'underground' movements of freedom fighters were resisting Japanese domination.

Another factor helped to make the Japanese unpopular. The early victories left them with thousands of civilian and military prisoners – far more than they had expected. Japanese soldiers believed it was dishonourable to surrender; far better to commit suicide. They despised soldiers who had given themselves up and often treated them very badly. Prisoners of war were made to labour hard in tropical

QUESTIONS

1 Why was time on the side of the United States in the Pacific war?

2 Why might some Asian peoples have welcomed the Japanese?

3 What factors help to explain the Japanese treatment of prisoners?

4 Although Germany and Japan were allies, they did not help each other during the war. Can you suggest reasons for this?

conditions on short rations. Thousands died of disease, starvation and overwork. Civilians, including women and children, were treated little better; many were confined in unhealthy prison-style camps **(Source 5)**.

Five minutes at Midway

President Roosevelt and his allies agreed almost at once that Germany was more powerful than Japan and therefore the greater danger. So the defeat of Hitler came first in all their plans; Russia did not join in the war against Japan but promised to do so once Hitler was defeated.

Nevertheless, powerful American naval forces were available to engage the Japanese. All the US aircraft carriers had escaped the destruction at Pearl Harbour. This was important because improvements in the range and performance of aircraft soon indicated that carriers, not battleships, would play the key role in future sea battles. On 10 December 1941 two of Britain's finest battleships, the *Prince of Wales* and *Repulse*, sailing without air-cover, were sunk by Japanese dive-bombers. Such a devastating blow showed that naval battles would be won or lost by ships letting loose not shells but aircraft at each other.

The first 'carrier to carrier' battle took place in May 1942 when the Japanese tried to capture the Solomon Islands and Port Moresby in Papua as 'stepping stones' for an invasion of Australia. The Japanese

SOURCE 6

This photograph was taken on the deck of the sinking British battleship *Prince of Wales*. Altogether 840 men died when the *Prince of Wales* and *Repulse* were sunk by the Japanese on 10 December 1941.

SOURCE 5

Phyllis Briggs was a nurse in Singapore. She was captured when a Japanese destroyer sank the ship in which she had escaped from the port.

The first night we lay on concrete slabs trying to sleep – the small children screamed all night and every hour a Jap guard tramped through our block and seemed to take delight in hitting our shins with the butt of his rifle ... One girl was brought in, the only survivor from a raft full of people ... She had reached a small island and after three days there she was taken off by a cargo boat which was ... sunk the same night. Four days later she was picked up by a Jap battleship ... she had survived all this time by collecting rainwater in the lid of her powder compact ... A British Air Force officer had to have a foot amputated [with] a saw made out of a knife ... Another man ... had been bayonetted in the stomach when trying to get a drink of water.

The Japanese aircraft carrier *Hiryu* in flames at the battle of Midway, 4 June 1942. Before it sank, the *Hiryu* managed to disable the US carrier *Yorktown*.

fleet's movements were known to American Intelligence which had cracked the Japanese war-code. Armed with this information, US warships and planes made a surprise attack on the Japanese fleet in the Coral Sea. The Japanese lost so many planes that they were forced to turn back.

This first defeat was followed by a disaster for the Japanese. In April 1942 the city of Tokyo had been bombed by American aircraft. The Japanese leaders were deeply insulted; they tortured, imprisoned and executed airmen shot down in the raid. The American bombers had been launched from a carrier but the Japanese were convinced that the planes must have come from the US-controlled Midway Island. In retaliation, they assembled a huge force – eleven battleships, eight carriers, and smaller vessels carrying 5000 troops – and sent it to capture the island. American Intelligence again knew all about the Japanese plans, so the stage was set for one of the biggest surprises of the war.

Believing that American warships were hundreds of miles away, the Japanese Admiral sent in bombers to 'soften up' Midway's defences in preparation for a landing. These planes had just returned to reload and refuel when waves of US planes arrived unexpectedly overhead. The Japanese carriers had planes, equipment and fuel pipes across their decks when US bombers dived on them **(Source 8)**. Within five minutes, three Japanese carriers were blazing wrecks, as burning petrol and exploding torpedoes and bombs tore them apart. As night fell, their flaming hulks lit up the sky until, one by one, they sank, taking 2000 men and 250 aircraft with them. Later, another Japanese carrier was destroyed, although the Americans also lost one of their own.

Those five fatal minutes at Midway changed the balance of power in the Pacific war. Without command of the sea and air, the Japanese could not keep open supply lines linking the different parts of their new empire with the homeland. US submarines and planes were able to destroy increasing

SOURCE 8

A Japanese sailor, T.V. Tuleja, describes the scene on the *Kaga*, one of the carriers destroyed at Midway.

The fire raced along rivulets of gasoline, spreading disaster below decks. Men trapped behind blistering bulkheads were roasted alive. Hoses rolled out in a frantic effort to hold back the flames caught fire. Some officers and men, their uniforms smouldering and their faces blackened by smoke, were driven back to the edge of the flight deck and from there they leaped into the sea. Then the fire travelled to the bomb storage lockers. Suddenly there was a thunderous explosion, and sheets of glowing steel were ripped like so much tin foil ... Great clouds of black smoke arose ...[smelling] of burning gasoline, paint, wood, rubber and human flesh.

numbers of Japanese merchant ships. Reduced supplies of food, fuel and raw materials meant that Japan's industries slowed down and its people suffered increasing hardship. Midway for the Japanese, like Stalingrad for the Germans, was the beginning of the end.

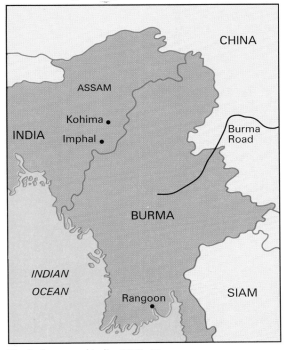

War in Burma and India, 1942–45

The war in Burma

The Japanese occupation of Burma cut off Allied communications with China. It also threatened British rule in India. For years Indians had been demanding independence from Britain. Should they now welcome the Japanese as 'liberators' and do their best to help overthrow the British **(Source 9)**? Fortunately for Britain, most Indians realised that the Japanese would not allow them to be free. Consequently, the thousands of Indians serving in the British forces remained loyal and fought bravely in Burma and elsewhere. A few, captured by the Japanese, joined an 'Indian National Army' set up by Japan to encourage rebellion against British rule.

The immediate task for the British was to open up the road through Burma used to supply the Chinese in their war against

SOURCE 10

Field Marshal William Slim, Britain's successful commander in Burma. He said of the enemy, 'Lots of soldiers talk about fighting to the last; only the Japanese do it'.

Japan. In 1943–44 a British and Indian army commanded by General William Slim fought a series of campaigns to open up the Burma road. There were no short cuts in fighting of this kind. Every yard of jungle, swamp, hill and mountain had to be taken from a brave and cunning enemy, often in hand-to-hand combat.

By March 1944 the British seemed set to open communications with China. The Japanese struck back by invading the Indian province of Assam. They surrounded a British army at Imphal, but Slim managed to supply the troops by air. Then the British, in turn, closed in on the Japanese. Cut off from their bases, the Japanese were soon short of food and ammunition. In a desperate, three-month battle around Kohima the Japanese army was destroyed. By January 1945 Slim had killed or captured three Japanese armies amounting to 347,000 men. He was ready to take Rangoon, the capital of Burma, and invade Malaya **(Source 11)**.

Japan fights to the last

The Americans, meanwhile, made steady progress across the Pacific, recapturing one island after another. When the Philippines fell, in October 1944, the oil supply route from the Dutch East Indies to Japan was cut. Desperately, the Japanese challenged the US navy to a battle in Leyte Gulf. In the largest naval battle in history, involving 282 warships, the Americans gained a terrible revenge for Pearl Harbour. Four Japanese carriers and two battleships were sunk,

SOURCE 11

This letter home from Burma was written by Peter Gadsdon, a British officer who fought in the advance on Rangoon.

21.3.45
Dear Mum and Dad,
Yesterday morning ... it became apparent that there was quite a battle in progress, mostly our stuff firing, so I crossed my fingers and in we went ... It turned out that we'd given the Jap a devil of a knock; there were forty-nine draped on the wire in front of us ... Every time one (a Japanese soldier) moved he was shot at, and a number were blowing themselves up with grenades ... To my delight I found an officer badly wounded but alive. He was made prisoner and sent back where I believe he gave information before he died.

SOURCE 12

US marines fight desperately to gain a foothold on the island of Iwo Jima in February 1945. They had expected to capture the eight square miles of Iwo Jima in a few days, but it took five weeks to overcome fierce resistance from over 20,000 Japanese dug into concealed trenches.

Michael Moynihan, a war correspondent for a national newspaper, sailed with the British Pacific Fleet during the last months of the war in the Far East. He wrote this on 9 May 1945.

Out of a clear evening sky Japanese *kamikazes* swooped ... The first two ...made for the same ship, an aircraft carrier. Both hit the flight deck and both by some lucky chance plunged from there into the sea, blazing wrecks . . . At the back of one's mind continually is the thought of the pilots – fanatical, cold-blooded, whose last ambition is that death might also be glory ... Of the death dive of a third *kamikaze* I had a breath-taking view ... He came up the centre of the flight deck ... and abruptly all was lost in a confusion of smoke and flame ... It seemed that the ship was doomed ... but within half an hour the flames were extinguished.

together with many smaller vessels. After such a defeat there was little the Japanese could do except fight and die. *Kamikaze* (suicide) pilots, locked in planes which were like flying bombs, dived straight on to enemy warships (**Sources 13 and 14**). Entire regiments killed themselves rather than surrender, or charged to certain death against massed machine-gun fire.

Fanatical resistance of this kind increased American losses. When Okinawa and Iwo Jima were captured, almost all the Japanese defenders were killed, but so too were 15,000 Americans. If islands hundreds of miles from Japan were defended to the last man, how would the Japanese fight when their homeland and the Emperor were threatened? The American government thought that losses of one million were possible, especially when news came that the Japanese were preparing to use *kamikaze* warships and to give weapons to the entire adult population.

A possible solution was to bomb Japan into surrender. Raids on Japanese cities had already reached devastating proportions. In March 1945 one raid by B29 Super-fortresses on Tokyo had killed 83,000 civilians (**Source 15**). But still Japan fought on. The answer to the Allies' problem finally came in midsummer – only days after the Japanese had asked the Russians to help them negotiate a peace.

A Japanese *kamikaze* suicide plane plunges into the Pacific Ocean after coming under fire from an American aircraft carrier. Altogether, *kamikaze* attacks sank 34 US ships and badly damaged 288 others.

SOURCE 15

Robert Guillan, a Frenchman, lived in Japan during the war. Here he describes what happened during the great 'firestorm' raid on Tokyo, 9 March 1945.

In the dense smoke, where the wind was so hot it seared (burned) the lungs, people struggled then burst into flames where they stood ... It was often their feet that began to burn first ... Hundreds of people crawled into holes for shelter; their charred bodies were found after the raid ... Wherever there was a canal, people hurled themselves into the water ... Hundreds ... were later found dead; not drowned, but suffocated by smoke. In other places, the water got so hot that ...they simply boiled alive.

SOURCE 16

The atomic bomb became possible when scientists led by Enrico Fermi set up a 'chain reaction', in which a split atom splits other atoms. One of those present described the moment in December 1942.

There was polite clapping. Then Fermi waved at us to come over and join him ... Eugene Wigner ... produced a bottle of Chianti (wine) ... There were no toasts, no speeches, but most signed the bottle ... For some time we had known we were about to unlock a giant; still, we could not escape an eerie feeling when we knew we had actually done it ... Leo Szilard ... shook hands with Fermi and said he thought it would go down as a black day in the history of mankind.

SOURCE 17

America's new President, Harry S. Truman (right), presents General Eisenhower with the Distinguished Service Medal (June 1945).

The beginnings of the atomic age

On 16 July 1945 scientists successfully tested a nuclear device at Los Alamos in the US state of New Mexico. For years it had been known that if an atom were split by bombardment from other atoms, the energy released would have enormous destructive power. In 1939 physicists who had escaped from Fascist-dominated Europe warned President Roosevelt of the danger if Nazi laboratories produced the bomb first. After the USA entered the war, Roosevelt set up a research centre at Oak Ridge, Tennessee. It was this centre, expanded over the years into a factory complex, which made the bomb tested at Los Alamos **(Source 16)**.

Roosevelt died in April 1945. His successor as President, Harry Truman, saw the bomb as a way of ending the war quickly and saving Allied lives. He was also deeply suspicious of Soviet Russia. Russian troops had taken over eastern Europe after the defeat of Hitler. Truman hoped to beat Japan without Russian help and so save Manchuria and the Far East from similar Communist occupations. When Truman met Stalin at Potsdam, near Berlin, on 24 July, he merely told him that the United States had 'a new weapon of unusual destructive force', little

SOURCE 18

A Swedish newspaper, *Aftonbladitt*, reported the attack on Hiroshima on 9 August 1945. Sweden had not been involved in the Second World War.

Although Germany began bomb warfare against open towns and civilian populations, all records ... have been beaten by the Anglo-Saxons (Americans and British) ... The so-called rules of warfare ... must brand the bombing of Hiroshima as a first class crime. It is all very well if atom raids shorten the war, but this experiment with the entire city as a 'guinea-pig' reflects no glory on its authors. The professors who thought out the whole thing can hardly feel any joy over the first application of their discovery.

SOURCE 20

General MacArthur of the USA receives the surrender of Japan on board the battleship *Missouri*, 2 September 1945. Japanese units throughout the Pacific signed similar surrender documents.

SOURCE 19

Laurens van der Post was a prisoner of the Japanese. Here he explains his point of view about the bomb.

If the atom bomb had not been dropped ... the war would have dragged on ... For me, selfish as it may sound, there was the certain knowledge that if the bomb had not been dropped ... hundreds of thousands of prisoners ... would have been killed ... Even if we had not been deliberately massacred we were near our physical end through lack of food.

QUESTIONS

1 In what ways was the battle of Midway a turning point?

2 Why did Chandra Bose (Source 9) want to remove the British from India with as little outside help as possible?

3 How did the Americans justify their use of the atomic bomb against Japan?

4 Why did President Truman try to prevent Stalin knowing about the atomic bomb?

knowing that the Soviet dictator knew all about the bomb from spies at Los Alamos!

On 3 August Truman told the chief of the air force to drop a bomb on Japan as soon as possible. The target chosen was Hiroshima, a city with a large military base **(Sources 18 and 19)**. Three days later, when no word had been heard from the Japanese, a second atomic device was exploded over Nagasaki. That day Russia declared war on Japan and the Red Army swarmed into Manchuria. Hirohito, Emperor of Japan, could stand his people's suffering no longer. In his first ever broadcast to his subjects he told them that they 'must bear the unbearable' and surrender.

The Japanese believed that their Emperor was a god – the 'Son of Heaven'. Few dared to disobey him, and there was no resistance when the Americans landed. However, hundreds of army officers killed themselves and *kamikaze* pilots took off and dived into Tokyo Bay as a last show of defiance to the enemy. On 2 September General Douglas MacArthur, the US Supreme Commander in the Pacific, received the Japanese surrender on the US battleship *Missouri*, anchored off Tokyo. At least fifty million people had died violently since Neville Chamberlain's Sunday broadcast six years earlier.

Assessment tasks

A Knowledge and understanding

1 a Summarise the main reasons for (i) Japan's military successes early in the war, and (ii) Japan's eventual defeat.
  b Are any of the reasons you have given for (i) and (ii) connected? Explain your answer.

2 a Ships and aircraft played a leading role in the war in the Far East. Give reasons for this.
  b Describe the changes that occurred at this time in the way ships and planes were used in warfare?

3 a Describe the different attitudes of the Japanese and the western Allies towards war.
  b What factors might help to explain these differences?

B Interpretations and sources

4 Here are some differing views about the dropping of atomic bombs on Japan in August 1945.

   The use of this barbarous weapon ... was of no assistance in our war against Japan. The Japanese were already defeated and were ready to surrender because of the sea blockade and successful bombing ... The scientists wanted to make this test because of the vast sums ... spent on the project. Truman knew that and so did the other people involved.
   (Admiral William Leahy, a wartime naval commander, 1974)

   I believe that we should have demonstrated it (the atomic bomb) to the Japanese before using it. Had we succeeded, had the Japanese surrendered after such a demonstration, then a new age would have started in which the power of human knowledge had stopped a war without killing a single individual ... We made a great mistake.
   (Edward Teller, one of the A-bomb scientists, 1974)

   More and more people see the horror of Hiroshima and Nagasaki ... as an act in which we (the Allies) alone were the villains. I have been amazed to observe how ... my own Japanese friends do not seem to feel that they had done anything themselves to provoke us into inflicting ... [the atomic bomb] on them.
   (Laurens van der Post, former Japanese prisoner of war, 1970)

   At that time the Army felt it would be a great shame to surrender ... The A-bomb provided an excellent spur (to surrender) because it sacrificed many people other than military men. This provided us with an excuse ... to cease the war to save ... innocent civilians. If the A-bomb had not been dropped we would have had great difficulty in finding a good reason to end the war.
   (Hisatune Sakomizu, secretary to Japan's war cabinet, 1974)

   a How far do you think each of these views was influenced by the background and experience of the writer?
   b Do you find any of these views unconvincing? If so, why?

5 How useful are Sources 2 and 15 in helping to explain the differences between a nuclear and non-nuclear bomb attack?

6 a Can we draw any conclusions about the Japanese treatment of prisoners from Source 4?
  b How reliable as historical evidence is this postcard? Give reasons for your answer.

7 The Home Front

The British at War, 1939–45

SOURCE 1

Rolf Atkinson, an evacuee from London, fits a light shield to a car headlamp – to meet blackout regulations (1939). The dressing on his face had nothing to do with the war; it resulted from his first attempt at shaving!

Friday 1 September 1939 was a day to remember. It saw the start of a 'blackout' in Britain. No lights were put on in streets or shops and householders covered their windows and doors with blankets so as not to present targets for bombers. At first it was too dark for safety. Road accidents soared, many of them involving pedestrians. After a few months the government allowed dimly-lit streetlamps and hooded headlights on motor vehicles. Nevertheless for the next six years anybody showing a light unnecessarily was prosecuted.

Evacuation

Also on that first Friday of September, children and mothers with babies were evacuated out of London and other cities into country areas. The aim was to reduce casualties once air-raids began. The evacuation was on a massive scale: at least one and a quarter million people were evacuated during the first three days of September; further movements brought the total up to about three million by the end of 1941.

Although the evacuation had been carefully planned, there was much confusion. Crowded trains moved slowly with frequent stops and diversions, sometimes reaching the wrong destinations. Tired children had little to eat except chocolate and buns. They were given drinks at stations or by people living near the lines. At journey's end, parents in the reception areas picked the evacuees they wanted from bewildered groups assembled in school or village halls (**Source 3**). Some children found a home only after being led from door to door.

This sudden uprooting of millions of people brought some surprises. For many evacuees it was their first sight of the country. Many were disappointed to find no street lights, Woolworths or fish and chip shops. Such was their ignorance of farming life that on one train two boys were heard arguing whether the animals they could see in a field were pigs or sheep. For some country families there were serious shocks. They found they had taken in dirty, ragged children who wet the bed at night and had never used a knife and fork. Angry mothers were soon swapping 'horror stories' of girls

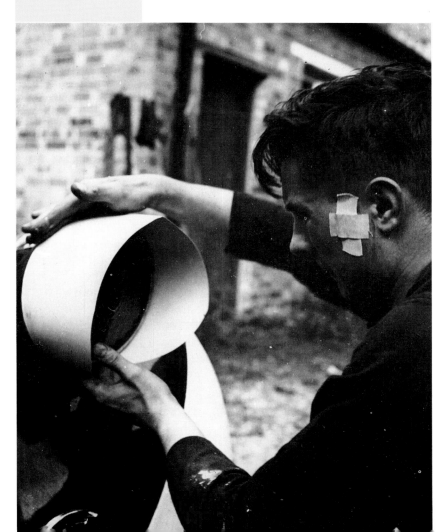

SOURCE 2

Young children being evacuated from London to the West Country. They are carrying gas masks and identification labels.

SOURCE 3

Doreen and William Holloway, from Battersea in London, were evacuated to Berkshire and found themselves in Binfield Village Hall.

We stood in a circle with our cases and packages. Some of the villagers came here to select children they wanted. It got so my brother and I were left till the last and I began to feel most unwanted and rejected because we seemed to be overlooked all the time. Nobody wanted a boy and a girl. At one point a man wanted to take me from my brother and I got very frightened. He wanted to take my clothes out of my case but I stopped him. But we were eventually taken to a home in the village.

SOURCE 4

This letter from F. Tennyson Jesse appeared in *The Times* newspaper on 22 September 1939.

Sir,

While from all my friends in the country comes praise of many town-children evacuees ... complaints are pouring in about the half-savage, verminous and wholly illiterate children from some slums. Stories ... are told of mattresses and carpets polluted, of wilful despoilation (dirtying) that one would only associate with untrained animals ... Now one hears that both women and children of the roughest and uncleanest types are going back to their 'homes' ... Let the mothers go back if they will ... but surely children should not be allowed to go back to conditions which shame a nation fighting for civilisation.

who never wore knickers and boys who did not bother to use a lavatory **(Source 4)**.

Most evacuees were no worse fed or clothed than country children. But a minority came from poor, inner-city areas. Better-off people were astonished at the state of these slum children. They were seeing for the first time just how badly the poorest members of society had been affected by the long-term unemployment of the 1930s. Although there were schemes of National Insurance covering some sick and unemployed workers, state social security in 1939 was patchy, often missing out those most in need.

In October, the government decided to make parents of evacuees contribute towards the cost of their upkeep. This accelerated the drift back home which had started when there were no immediate air attacks. Of those who left London in September, 900,000 had returned to the capital by Christmas. Later in the war, after bombing began, there were other evacuations, often disorganised and caused by panic, fear and homelessness. But Britain never again saw a mass movement of the kind that began on 1 September 1939.

The Home Guard

On 14 May 1940 the government appealed for men between the ages of 17 and 65 to join the LDV (Local Defence Volunteers). The response was immediate and overwhelming **(Source 5)**. Over 250,000 men signed on in the first 24 hours, many of them ex-soldiers who had served in the First World War.

The LDV – some said the letters stood for 'Look, Duck and Vanish' – was renamed the Home Guard in August. By then Britain was in danger of invasion. Its only regular (full-time) army had been brought back from Dunkirk (see page 39) with hardly any weapons and equipment. The Home Guard was an essential part of the country's defences until new armies could be trained and equipped. Its men had no uniforms – just denim overalls or armbands – and their weapons varied from old rifles to pitchforks, sporting guns, pikes and, in one reported case, a chair leg **(Source 7)**.

SOURCE 5

The response to the government's call for Local Defence Volunteers (later called the Home Guard) was overwhelming. Here an officer describes the enrolment in Birmingham.

The weather was sweltering and we were allotted a small ... room in the police station yard ... Applicants ... started to queue up as soon as they could leave work and by 11 pm there were still scores of them waiting to enrol. Every night we worked until the small hours of the morning ... Within a few days the platoon was three or four hundred strong and it seemed ... all the male population of Birmingham would be enrolled within a week or two.

SOURCE 7

Just before Christmas 1940, the commander of the Home Guard in Bideford, Devon, sent this message to his troops.

We have certain grounds for congratulating ourselves. Half the trying autumn-winter season is behind us ... And now the shortest day is past the Black-out time will gradually get shorter ... But there is no room for complacency ... The enemy is conscious that with every day that passes our military strength increases. He is bound to try ... [to attack] our main citadel – Britain herself ... It is up to us to hold the fort, to defend this Ancient Castle (Britain) ... The battlements are manned, the portcullis is down, the drawbridge is up, and I give you as your motto ... 'look to your moat'.

SOURCE 6

A member of the Home Guard at Watford in Hertfordshire gives rifle instruction to a volunteer in the local Women's Home Defence Unit.

Such a force could not have held back the Germans for long. However it performed useful work guarding bridges, road junctions and other key points. It stopped unnecessary movements on the roads and kept an eye open for spies and other suspicious characters. A real worry at the time was that the Germans might drop paratroopers to spread disorder and disruption, as they had done in Holland and Belgium. The Home Guard, on the lookout for such aerial invaders, often raised false alarms; one unit mistook a flock of swans landing in a sunset for the enemy.

After the victory of the RAF in the Battle of Britain the danger of invasion faded and some of the early enthusiasm for the Home Guard died away. Nevertheless, from November 1940 the Home Guard was organised as an army, with ranks, and modern weapons and equipment. Its members had to attend drills, parades and exercises and, after 1942, they were even conscripted (forced to join).

QUESTIONS

1 Long after the war, the Home Guard was given the name 'Dad's Army.' In what ways is this a suitable description?

2 What did the author of Source 7 mean when he told his troops to 'look to your moat'?

3 What advantages were to be gained by bombing cities at night?

4 Why were well-to-do people unlikely to be found sheltering in an Underground station (Source 12)?

SOURCE 8

The Home Guard kept a lookout for suspicious persons, including survivors from shot-down enemy planes. In this training exercise, a man dressed as a woman pretends to shoot a guard at a roadblock.

The Blitz

Massed air attacks started on 7 September 1940 – a year after the first evacuation. At 5 o'clock on that Saturday evening 300 German aircraft flew to London, using the river Thames as a guide. Their targets were a cluster of docks, warehouses, factories and homes to the north of the river, and the Woolwich Arsenal, a big government armament factory, on the south bank. Stored in the busy docklands were large amounts of wood, food, wine, spirits, wool, tar and cotton. When the Germans dropped high explosive and incendiary (fire) bombs, fires broke out almost immediately. A huge blanket of black and grey smoke, lit by the brightly coloured flames of burning rubber and timber, rose high into the air and spread over ten miles **(Source 9)**.

That afternoon, around five o' clock, I went outside the house. I'd heard the aircraft ... the first formations were coming over ... very, very majestic, terrific ... I had no thought they were actually bombers. Then I became well aware, because bombs began to fall, and shrapnel was ... dancing off the cobbles. Then the ... suction and compression from the high explosive blasts just pulled ... and pushed you ... You could actually feel your eyeballs being sucked out. I was holding my eyes to try to stop them going. And the suction ripped my shirt away, and ripped my trousers. Then I couldn't get my breath; the smoke was like acid and everything around me was black and yellow.

Choking fumes overcame many firemen. Flaming alcohol ran through some streets. Rats, driven in their thousands from burning warehouses, ran across roads and gardens. A mess of sugar, soap and tar dripped into the river, making it seem that the water itself was on fire. By 7.30 pm, when fresh bombers arrived, the fires were out of control and people were being evacuated by boat. Hundreds of Londoners were killed and thousands more made homeless. Next morning the survivors were given temporary shelter at Rest Centres, usually schools, in the suburbs.

'Black Saturday' was the start of the Blitz (the word comes from the German *Blitzkrieg* – see page 36). For 67 nights, with only one break, the *Luftwaffe* bombed London, hoping to break the spirit of its citizens **(Source 11)**. Night after night people went to their Anderson shelters in the garden or slept in public shelters or Underground railway stations **(Source 12)**. On 14 November the Germans switched to Coventry, where they destroyed the city centre with its ancient cathedral. Heavy night raids on other cities followed.

The Blitz ended in May 1941 when the *Luftwaffe* moved its bases east for the invasion of Russia (see page 41). Isolated bombing raids continued until June 1944 when a fresh ordeal began for Londoners. Hitler ordered V1s – new, pilotless flying bombs – to be fired at London in retaliation for the heavy bombing of Germany (see

SOURCE 11

During the Blitz, Mrs Joan Veazey, newly married to a church curate in south London, kept a diary by jotting notes on a pad attached by a rubber band to her wrist. Here are some extracts.

16 September
Another bad night, with bombs falling and guns firing incessantly … It is very eerie going round the rooms on the top floor when … a plane seems to be hovering just over the roof … They must have broken the gas and water mains last night because there is no gas and no water.

17 September
We didn't have a moment's rest last night. The Germans came over in waves… There have been many terrible casualties by bombing but we cannot know the numbers yet because the press keep everything so vague in case of giving the enemy any information.

18 September
I was busy frying the breakfast egg this morning when I noticed through the window a German plane coming in to bomb. Suddenly I saw three black blobs leave the plane. I landed flat on my tummy, still holding the frying pan.

SOURCE 12

Emily Eary was a Londoner who spent her nights in the Underground. Many of its stations became permanent shelters, with bunks.

In the evenings you'd get ladies and gentlemen going home after the theatre and night-club people. And you felt they were staring and sneering at you, as much to say 'Look at them'. You'd be there on the platform, putting your curlers in or whatever, and you felt a bit humiliated … We were a bit resentful about it, what with them going back to their safe areas and their comfortable homes. They didn't have to go through what we did.

SOURCE 13

London Transport installed bunkbeds in some Underground tube stations. Here we see shelterers sleeping at Holborn station while passengers wait for the last train of the day (January 1941).

The scene at Clapham in London on 17 June 1944 after a German V1 flying bomb had exploded. Inset: A flying bomb on its way to England. Altogether, 2350 of these so-called 'doodlebugs' fell on London, killing about 5000 people.

page 52). Some of these so-called 'doodlebugs' were shot down, but most reached their targets where they caused thousands of deaths and immense damage (Source 15). In September, an even deadlier weapon, the V2 rocket-bomb, was launched at the capital. Rising to a height of 60 miles and reaching speeds of 3600 mph, these missiles gave no warning sound like the V1s. There was no time to take shelter so casualties were heavy. Thousands of V2s fell on London until March 1945, when their continental launching sites were captured by Allied troops.

SOURCE 15

Lionel King, living in Leyton, east London, was eight years old when Hitler's V1s began to fall. This account, written nearly 30 years later, is based on a diary he kept at the time.

On the night of 12 June... news spread in from the Kent and Sussex coasts of aircraft with 'jet nozzles', 'fire exhausts' and odd engine sounds... The first came over one afternoon... It gave us little warning. Ten seconds and the engine cut out directly overhead. There was an oddly resounding explosion about half a mile away... Soon so many V1s were coming over the authorities gave up air raid warnings. They would have been sounding the siren all the time.

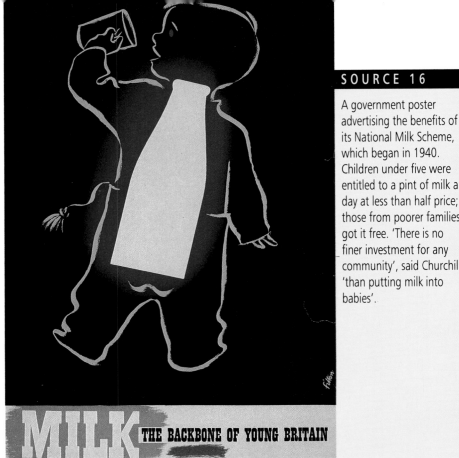

MILK THE BACKBONE OF YOUNG BRITAIN

Warfare and welfare

The coming of war exposed Britain's social problems. The evacuation in particular showed up the distressing slum conditions in many big cities. War also created new problems. As children were sent away, men were called up to fight and women went out to work, there was widespread disruption of family life and often increased hardship.

Existing schemes of social security were inadequate at the best of times. Old age pensions had been paid since 1908. But National Insurance payments to the sick and unemployed were for short periods only. Extra money for the long-term unemployed, known as 'the dole', could be claimed from an Unemployment Assistance Board, but only after a 'means test' in which every detail of the family's income was investigated. Health insurance only covered workers, not their families, and was for doctor care, not hospital treatment. The poorest members of the community remained at risk, especially if jobless or ill.

As the familiar props of everyday life fell away, the government was forced to step in. Money was made available for local education authorities to deal with serious cases of neglect amongst schoolchildren. At the same time evacuated children who needed medical care were treated free of charge. The Assistance Board dropped 'unemployment' from its title to indicate its

QUESTIONS

1. There is evidence that many British people were better fed and healthier during the war. Can you suggest reasons for this?

2. What was the point of rationing clothing during the war?

3. Why were identity cards thought necessary in wartime?

4. Look at Source 21. What was it trying to make women feel about war-work?

wider role in helping all in need, not just the jobless. During the air-raids, for example, it gave help to bombed-out families. From 1940, the Board issued supplementary (extra) pensions to elderly people and widows hit by wartime price rises. The state also provided milk and meals for schoolchildren, and vitamin supplements such as orange juice and cod liver oil for younger children, as part of its drive to protect the health of a nation at war.

In 1942 the government set up a committee, headed by Sir William Beveridge, to suggest ways of improving social security. Its report proposed a nationwide social insurance system which would benefit every man, woman and child. In return for weekly payments by employers and workers, a complete package of old age and widows' pensions, child, maternity and funeral allowances and unemployment and sick pay would be available. These proposals caught the public imagination **(Source 17)**. The Beveridge Report became a best-seller, even though its language was not easy to understand.

In films and public speeches, Beveridge stressed his belief that the threat of poverty could be overcome once and for all. To those on the 'home front' his report held out the promise of a better future after the war. To those in the armed forces, it seemed to offer something to fight for – a Welfare State.

Wartime shortages

Before the war Britain had imported well over half its food and raw materials. Consequently the U-boat campaign against Allied shipping (see page 52) meant that many necessities were scarce throughout the war. The best way of ensuring equal shares for all is by rationing goods which are in short supply. The most vital commodity, petrol, was rationed in September 1939. After 1942 there were no supplies for private motorists, only for those on essential work such as nurses, farmers and doctors. Rationing of food

SOURCE 17

James Griffiths, a Labour MP, said this about the Beveridge Report during debates in the House of Commons in 1943.

The Beveridge Plan has become in the minds of the people ... a symbol of the kind of Britain we are determined to build when the victory is won, a Britain in which the mass of the people shall be ... [secure] from preventable want... Every comment in the press ... since the Report was issued ... [and] the widespread interest taken in it ... are clear indications that ... the plan meets a deep-felt need in the minds and hearts of the people.

SOURCE 18

Sir William (later Lord) Beveridge. His 1942 report on social insurance became the basis for Britain's Welfare State after the war.

started on 3 January 1940 with ham, bacon, sugar and butter. Later, meat, tea, jam and marmalade were added.

Clothes rationing began in May 1941. This often made it hard for mothers to clothe their children, let alone think of dressing fashionably themselves. It was reported that one wartime wedding dress was worn by seven brides! Stockings were in such short supply that young women often painted their legs brown when going out for the evening. Sweets, because of their high sugar content, were scarce from the start of the war and kept 'under the counter' for regulars by many shopkeepers. Official rationing of sweets began in 1942.

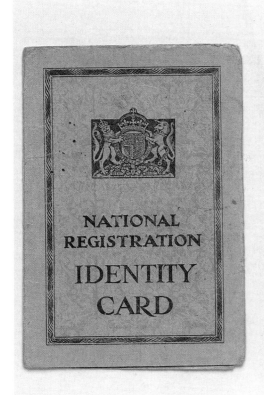

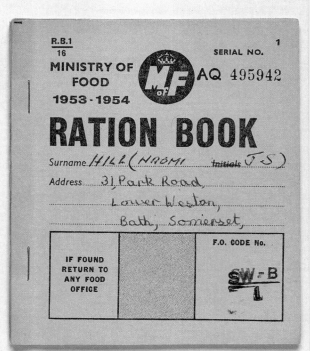

An identity card – all people carried them during the war – and ration book. The pages of the ration book were divided into small coupons which were cut out by the shopkeeper when the goods were purchased.

The government's Ministry of Information put out posters encouraging people to avoid waste and save energy. Two Ministry characters, Dr Carrot and Potato Pete, were created to give useful cooking hints. Dr Carrot suggested recipes which used little rationed food, such as carrot jam, sardine pancakes, rabbit pudding and chestnut soup. In one information leaflet, Potato Pete suggested ways of cooking sparrow pie. Another campaign, 'Dig for Victory', encouraged the digging up of parkland and playing fields to grow food crops. Even roadside verges were planted with rows of potatoes.

Few people lived entirely on their weekly rations. Most ate in cafés, restaurants or factory canteens at least once a day. Schoolchildren were given lunches at subsidised prices – or free in cases of need. Meanwhile many people found they could get food and other articles illegally on the 'black market' (**Source 20**).

Women at war

With so many men away on war service, women were needed to take over jobs of all kinds. From 1941, all women had to register at government offices if they were between the ages of 17 and 49 and unmarried or without a young family. If the job they were doing was considered inessential they were directed into work 'of national importance', even if this meant leaving home.

Women went to work in heavy industries such as chemicals, engineering, steel and munitions. They made tanks, guns, shells, lorries, jeeps and aircraft. They worked on buses, trains and in the shipyards. They drove fire-engines and ambulances, worked as nurses, air-raid wardens, mechanics, dispatch-riders and wireless operators. The Women's Land Army took on the rough, dirty and often back-breaking task of helping farmers grow the extra food

You'd go into your grocer's and he'd say, 'Got some peaches' or 'Got some corned beef today', or whatever was rationed or unavailable. You'd make an offer as to what you'd pay for it; it was always above the normal price. You could buy coupons for food or clothing off workmates, or perhaps from spivs (dishonest traders) in pubs. The whole thing was causing a lot of bad feeling and resentment. If you did an under-the-counter deal, you wouldn't tell anyone who wasn't a close friend.

needed. This work involved long hours, frequently in primitive conditions and sometimes under air attack **(Source 22)**.

Many women joined organisations attached to the army, navy and air force: the ATS (Auxiliary Territorial Service), the WRNS (Women's Royal Naval Service) and the WAAF (Women's Auxiliary Air Force). Servicewomen had to obey the same strict rules as soldiers, sailors and airmen. Uniforms had to be clean, well-pressed and tidy; hair short and worn off the collar; buttons and shoes polished and shiny. Women learnt the same parade-ground drill as men, although without carrying rifles.

WOMEN OF BRITAIN
COME INTO THE FACTORIES
ASK AT ANY EMPLOYMENT EXCHANGE FOR ADVICE AND FULL DETAILS

SOURCE 21

A government recruiting poster from March 1941. It accompanied a scheme of the Minister of Labour, Ernest Bevin, to recruit an extra 100,000 women for war work. To this end there was a big expansion in day and night nurseries for young children.

SOURCE 22

Miss M.H. Bigwood went to work as a Land Girl on a Welsh farm.

The farmer belittled everything I did. 'What can a girl like you do on a farm?' ... In spite of this, I was interested in the work ... The only chance of a bath was to use the old butter tub, dragged upstairs, filled with pails of ... [boiling] water ... We used to go to the village fortnightly hops (dances) ... We all wore evening dresses; pinned up and often with our heavy macs on and in pouring rain [we would] cycle ... 3 miles to town.

Like the men they were punished for the slightest disobedience by extra duties and loss of free time **(Source 23)**.

Servicewomen carried out both clerical and technical duties. Their work was often dangerous. The ATS operated anti-aircraft guns and searchlights. WAAF units handled the large, clumsy barrage balloons which were put up to prevent low-level air attacks. A WAAF radar operator who stayed at her post during an air-raid became the only servicewoman to win the Military Medal for bravery. Altogether, 700 servicewomen were killed 'on active service' during the war. A particularly dangerous job was carried out by women pilots who delivered new planes from factories to airfields.

Despite a great deal of discomfort and danger, war service gave many women skills and experience they would not otherwise have acquired. Their efforts during the Second World War helped to inspire future generations of women in their struggle for equal opportunities with men.

SOURCE 23

D.J. 'Panda' Carter remembers her introduction to life in the Auxiliary Territorial Service (ATS).

We were to live twenty-four to a hut ... In my hut ... were two girls ... who had to have their heads shaved because they had lice. One poor soul ... wet the bed ... An Irish ballet dancer ... screamed and shouted in the middle of the night and sometimes walked in her sleep ... At 5.30 am we started ... by lining up to be given work. It consisted of cleaning toilets, scrubbing floors ... lighting fires ... Our four weeks' training were like a complete new world. Each day ... when the camp was ship-shape, we spent many hours learning to march and obey commands. I enjoyed it after a while ... we had learnt discipline.

SOURCE 24

In this painting by Dame Laura Knight we see members of the Women's Auxiliary Air Force handling a barrage balloon. Such balloons, held in the sky with wire cables reaching the ground, prevented enemy pilots from flying low.

Assessment tasks

A Knowledge and understanding

1 a List ways in which the war affected the lives of civilians in Britain.
  b Which of these effects were purely short-term (for the duration of the war only) and which had longer-term consequences? Give reasons for your answer.

2 Why and how did the war spur the British government to take greater responsibility for people's welfare?

3 a Why was rationing introduced during the war?
  b What were the attitudes of the British people towards rationing?

B Interpretations and sources

4 Historians disagree about the usefulness of the Local Defence Volunteers – the 'Home Guard'.

What contribution did the Home Guard make to victory? … In the summer of 1940 … [it] helped to inspire the whole country and to transform the national attitude to the war. The LDV's first duties … of observing and reporting were useful and sensible; the real fighting was to be left to the Army.
(Norman Longmate, 1974)

The Home Guard was to play a key role in the defence of London's … anti-tank lines. It was stressed at the time (1940) that these lines should be held to the last man … A number of Spanish civil war veterans … set up a school to train Home Guards in … the use of Molotov Cocktails (petrol bombs) … camouflage and street fighting … [and] to demobilise tanks.
(Joanna Mack & Steve Humphries, 1985)

There were few rifles to spare for it (the LDV) until the late summer and, even when these were issued, there was no ammunition. The Home Guard harassed innocent civilians for their identity cards, put up primitive road blocks … and sometimes made bombs out of petrol tins. In a serious invasion, its members would presumably have been massacred if they had managed to assemble at all.
(A.J.P. Taylor, 1965)

  a What do these writers agree and disagree about?
  b Disagreements of this kind are hard to settle. Why?
  c Which account do you find the most convincing, and why?

5 a From the written sources in this chapter, can you find any evidence that the hardships of war were not equally shared by the British people?
  b How useful are this chapter's sources in giving a picture of life in wartime?

6 What do Sources 16 and 21 tell you about the Government's attitude towards the people? How might such campaigns be conducted today? Give reasons for your answer.

Crime and Punishment

Mass murder during the Second World War

In February 1943, Ivan Krivozertsev, a farmer at Gniezdovo in German-occupied Russia, told the local Nazi Commander that there was a mass grave in the nearby Katyn forest. German troops went to the spot and uncovered the bodies of 4500 Polish officers and one woman, many of them still in uniform. All had had their hands tied behind their backs before being shot in the head – a usual method of Soviet execution.

The Katyn massacre

Diaries and letters found in the grave showed that all the victims had died early in 1940, over a year before Russia and Germany went to war **(Source 2)**. Obviously this was a crime carried out by Stalin's executioners. The Germans did their best to spread the news of their discovery and so blacken the reputation of Russia in the eyes of the world. They

SOURCE 1

Some of the bodies uncovered at Katyn forest. This picture was taken in 1943.

The Polish officers had been unaware of their fate until the last moment. Here is the final entry in the diary of Major Adam Solski, dated 9 April 1940.

A few minutes before five in the morning: reveille (wake-up call) in the prison train. Preparing to get off. We are to go somewhere by car. What next? ... Ever since dawn, the day has run an exceptional course. Departure in prison van with tiny cell-like compartments. Horrible. Driven somewhere into the woods ... Here a detailed search. I was relieved of my watch, which showed 6.30 a.m., asked for my wedding ring. Roubles, belt and penknife taken away.

KATYN
1940

SUMIENIE SWIATA WOLA O SWIADECTWO PRAWDZIE

IN REMEMBRANCE

OF 14,500 POLISH PRISONERS OF WAR WHO DISAPPEARED IN 1940
FROM CAMPS AT KOZIELSK, STAROBIELSK & OSTASZKOW OF WHOM
4,500 WERE LATER IDENTIFIED IN MASS-GRAVES AT KATYN NEAR SMOLENSK

SOURCE 3

This memorial to the Katyn dead was erected by Polish people living in London. It stands in Gunnersbury Cemetery, West London.

published photographs, letters and other documents and arranged for experts from countries not at war to visit the site.

Stalin denied all the charges. Instead, he blamed the Nazis for the killings, which he said had occurred in 1943. Roosevelt and Churchill, whatever their private doubts, accepted the Soviet version of events. Russia was the ally of Britain and the United States and its army was bearing the full force of the German onslaught. In any case, there seemed little reason to believe the Nazis whose own crimes against the Poles were well known.

Why did Stalin order these executions? Most of the dead were well-educated and talented – in peacetime they had been doctors, lawyers, scientists, writers and artists. They belonged to a class which would resist any attempt to make Poland Communist after the war. The executions were well organised and must have taken weeks to complete. Only the grave at Katyn was ever found but more than 15,000 Polish officers captured during the Soviet occupation disappeared at this time. After Russia recaptured the region in 1944 it became impossible to find out the truth.

Ivan Krivozertsev fled to England to escape the Red Army and Stalin's vengeance. In October 1947 he was found hanged at his Bristol home. The verdict was suicide, but did Stalin's agents get him after all?

The Final Solution

The massacre of the Poles was the first of many crimes of this kind during the Second World War. The Japanese, as we have seen, had no respect for their prisoners of war. Hitler was so furious at Italy's surrender in 1943 that he ordered 5000 Italian soldiers to be shot. But the worst crime of all was the mass murder of nearly six million Jews by the Nazis – now known as the Holocaust.

Nazi hatred of the Jews was well known (see page 8). Before the war Hitler had made the lives of German Jews unbearable by restricting their rights as citizens.

Thousands had fled from the country, leaving their property to be seized by Nazi supporters. The German conquests of 1940 and 1941, particularly in Poland and Russia, brought millions more Jews under Nazi rule. These unfortunate people could not escape. Many were shot straight away (Source 4). Most were confined to the poorer parts of cities or herded together in concentration camps while the Nazis decided what to do with them.

In 1942 Hitler ordered what he called 'the final solution of the Jewish problem'. They were to be wiped out so that their land and property could be taken over by 'racially pure' Aryans (Germans) (Source 6). The task of carrying out the 'Final Solution' was given to Heinrich Himmler, head of the *Gestapo* (German secret police). Himmler decided that the old, young, weak and sick were to be killed as soon as possible. People in better health would be worked hard first, then murdered (Source 7). Executions were to be swift, cheap and efficient. The rough and ready shootings of the early days were replaced by carefully planned mass killings in gas chambers.

Special 'death camps' were set up all over Germany and Poland (see map). At the Polish camps death was mass-produced as if in a factory. The victims arrived in cattle-trucks from all over occupied Europe. Many had died on the way; the survivors were dazed, starving and sick. Those unfit to work were told to strip for a shower. The

QUESTIONS

1 Why did it take so long for the truth to come out about the Katyn massacre?

2 What did Hitler mean when he spoke of the Jews 'bleeding' other people (Source 6)?

3 In what way does Source 7 help to explain the Nazis' treatment of the Jews?

4 Why did the Nazis set up their gas chambers in Poland rather than Germany?

SOURCE 4

Jan Karski, a Polish Jew, escaped to the West. Here he describes the methods of Nazi 'security battalions' in Warsaw.

The Jews, when caught, are driven into a square. Old people and cripples are then singled out, taken to the cemetery and there shot. The remaining people are loaded into goods trucks at the rate of 150 people to a truck with space for 40. The floor of the truck is covered with a thick layer of lime and chlorine sprinkled with water. The doors of the trucks are locked. Sometimes the train starts immediately, sometimes it remains on a siding for ... two days or even longer. The people are packed so tightly that [they] die of suffocation or from the fumes of lime and chlorine, from lack of air, water and food. Wherever the train arrives half the people are dead.

SOURCE 5

A Polish Jew about to be shot in the head by a German soldier (1942). Other Jews lie dead in the trench they have just dug.

SOURCE 6

In 1941 Hitler said this to a large crowd in Berlin.

The war will not end as the Jews imagine it will, namely with the uprooting of the Germans ... The result ... will be the complete extermination of the Jews. Now for the first time they will not bleed other people ... The old Jewish law of 'An eye for an eye, a tooth for a tooth' will be applied ... The further this war spreads, the further will spread this fight against ... the Jew.

SOURCE 7

Heinrich Himmler explains his attitude towards other peoples in a speech made on 4 October 1943.

Whether nations live in prosperity or starve to death interests me only in so far as we need them as slaves ... Whether 10,000 Russian females fall down from exhaustion while digging an anti-tank ditch for Germany interests me only in so far as the anti-tank ditch is dug ... If somebody comes to me and says: 'I cannot dig the anti-tank ditch with women and children, it is inhuman, it would kill them', then I have to say, 'You are the murderer of your own blood, for if the anti-tank ditch is not dug ... German soldiers will die'.

SOURCE 8

Heinrich Himmler, head of Hitler's Gestapo. He organised the death of millions, yet the only time he is known to have witnessed a shooting he fainted.

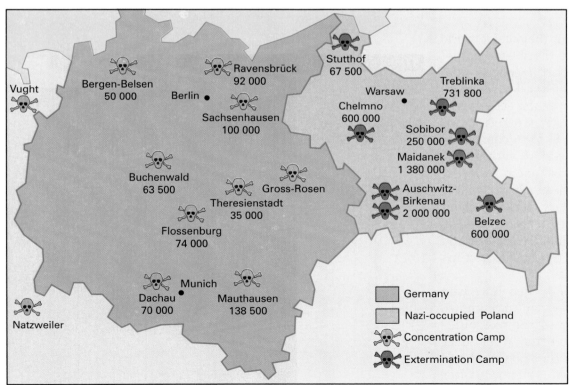

The Nazi death camps

The map shows the most notorious of the Nazi death camps. The figures of deaths in each are approximate; the exact number of people who died in these camps will never be known.

Stutthof 67 500
Ravensbrück 92 000
Bergen-Belsen 50 000
Berlin
Vught
Warsaw
Treblinka 731 800
Chelmno 600 000
Sachsenhausen 100 000
Sobibor 250 000
Maidanek 1 380 000
Buchenwald 63 500
Gross-Rosen
Theresienstadt 35 000
Auschwitz-Birkenau 2 000 000
Flossenburg 74 000
Belzec 600 000
Dachau 70 000
Munich
Mauthausen 138 500
Natzweiler

Germany
Nazi-occupied Poland
Concentration Camp
Extermination Camp

'showers' were actually gas chambers which could accommodate up to 2000 at a time.

Anyone who resisted was shot or driven into the chambers. Children were allowed to play until the last moment. The killing took about three minutes. 'We knew the people were dead because the screaming stopped', said the Commandant of Auschwitz. Corpses were used to help the German war effort. Gold teeth were sent to the German National Bank; during one 'busy' 15-day period in 1944 the guards at Auschwitz collected 40 kilograms of gold. Hair was shaved off and made into mattresses and flesh melted down for fat. What remained was burned in specially designed ovens. The ashes were scattered over the countryside or in rivers.

A great deal of this work was done by prisoners who were given extra food and a few more months of life as a reward. Operations were on a vast scale. The whole Auschwitz complex covered fifteen square miles and contained, besides huts, gas chambers and crematoria, factories making synthetic (artificial) petrol and rubber.

Who knew the truth?

Did the German people or the outside world know at the time about the death camps? The Nazis made little effort to conceal what they were doing in Poland and Russia but in western Europe they kept their activities as secret as possible. Jews in western cities and towns were invited to form councils to co-operate with the German authorities. These councils were instructed to select young, fit Jews from their neighbourhood to travel east to do 'voluntary work' in labour camps. These 'volunteers' were never seen again, although occasionally letters and postcards arrived, written by the victims and dated after their deaths.

Having got rid of able-bodied Jews who might have made trouble had they known the truth, it was easy to remove older people, women and children. Week after week the trains left on their journeys and only gradually did dreadful rumours filter back home. Had all these Jews been killed? It seemed unbelievable, and few suspected the truth. Certainly Jewish councils were still co-operating with the Germans when two prisoners, Rudolf Vrba and Fred Wetzler, escaped from Auschwitz in April 1944. The two men reached Switzerland where they wrote an account of their experiences **(Source 9)**. By July, this report had been read by Roosevelt and Churchill and its contents were known to many others.

SOURCE 9

Here is part of the report on the treatment of the Jews in Auschwitz prepared by Vrba and Wetzler and received in London on 4 July 1944. Oswieczim is the Polish name for Auschwitz.

At the end of February 1943, four new crematoria were built. Each crematorium contains a large hall, a gas chamber and a furnace. People are assembled in the hall which holds 2000 and gives the impression of a swimming-bath. They have to undress and are given a piece of soap and a towel as if they were going to the baths. Then they are crowded into the gas chamber which is ... sealed ... Gas is poured in through openings in the ceiling ... At the end of three minutes all the persons are dead. The ... bodies are taken away in carts to the furnace ... Only Jews are put to death by gas ... Aryans (non-Jews) are shot with pistols on special execution grounds between blocks 10 and 11 of Oswieczim camp.

SOURCE 10

The entrance to a gas chamber at Auschwitz concentration camp.

There could now be little doubt that the death camps existed – even though many believed the reports to be exaggerated **(Source 11)**. Some people in Britain and the United States demanded that 'something be done'. Would it be possible to bomb the railways leading to the camps, or even the camps themselves? Allied air chiefs were not in favour of such schemes. Auschwitz and the other Polish camps were a long way from air bases in western Europe; there might be heavy losses on such missions. An attack on the camps might provoke the Germans into speeding up the killing. The best way to save camp victims, claimed the experts, was to end the war as quickly as possible. Consequently only one camp, at Monowitz, was ever raided, and then it was to destroy its synthetic oil plant. The planes which carried out this attack flew within a few miles of Auschwitz.

When Russian, British and American troops liberated the camps the full horror was revealed. At Belsen, early in 1945, the British found 10,000 unburied bodies and starving people dying at the rate of 500 a day. The hunt for the guilty began at once.

Anne Frank and the 'Secret Annexe'

Anne Frank was a German Jew whose family fled to Amsterdam in the Netherlands when Hitler came to power. After the Germans occupied the country in 1940, Dutch Jews were at first subjected to numerous restrictions. They were made to wear yellow stars on their clothing to show they were Jews, forbidden to use trams, ride bicycles, go to the cinema or even sit in their gardens after eight o'clock at night.

SOURCE 11

In an interview after the war, Rudolf Vrba said this about people's reactions to his report.

If the Jews could not bring themselves to face the unbearable truth ... of Auschwitz, it is scarcely to be expected that the rest of the world would do so. Articles and broadcasts by those in a position to know ... attempted to put the truth across ... Fearful rumours, people said, but of course exaggerated ... Human beings – even the Nazis – could not behave like that ... The truths about the exterminations were of such a nature that it would inevitably take time for them to be absorbed by those who had never seen a concentration camp.

SOURCE 12

Here we see two of the survivors found by US troops at Buchenwald concentration camp (1945).

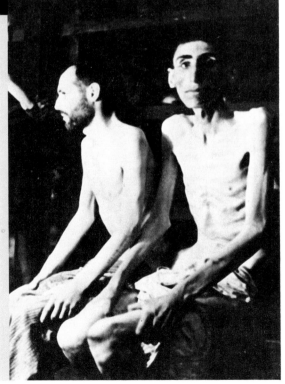

SOURCE 13

Anne Frank pictured just before she went into hiding.

In June 1942, soon after Anne's thirteenth birthday, the Nazis began to round up all the Jews in Amsterdam for transportation to the death camps. To save his family, Otto Frank, Anne's father, arranged for them to hide in the back rooms of the warehouse where he worked. These rooms were reached by a door concealed behind a bookcase and few people, except the owners of the building, knew they were there. This 'Secret Annexe', as Anne called it, was just large enough to accommodate Anne, her father, mother and sister Margot, Mr and Mrs Van Daan, their son Peter and a dentist named Dussel.

It must have seemed a desperate, almost hopeless gamble as they hurried from their home that day. 'Only when we were on the road did Mummy and Daddy begin to tell me bits and pieces about the plan', Anne wrote in the diary Otto had given her for her birthday. It meant never going out, never being seen or heard and living in cramped, unhealthy conditions without proper toilets. Yet Anne made it bearable by writing about

SOURCE 14

The outside of the building in Amsterdam where the Frank family and their friends hid for two years, and the bookcase which concealed the entrance to the 'Secret Annexe'.

it (Source 15). Peter Van Daan seemed to her, 'a rather soft, gawky youth' who arrived with his pet cat which soon spread fleas. Peter's mother, whom Anne grew to dislike, brought a chamber pot hidden in a hat-box. The hideaways lived on food smuggled in by friends. It was often little more than spinach, lettuce, dry bread and 'sweet, rotten potatoes'. 'Whoever wants a slimming course should stay in the Secret Annexe', wrote Anne.

The long silences were broken by BBC news, listened to on a crackling radio. The D-Day landings cheered them all up, and so did 'a speech by our beloved Winston Churchill'. Hopes that the war might soon end were mingled with fright as Allied bombers attacked the city in increasing numbers. Many buildings were destroyed and once Anne peeped out to see two airmen parachute from a burning plane. A constant worry were the burglars who often broke into the building at night. What if they

SOURCE 15

In April 1944, when burglars broke into the building where the Franks were hiding, the police searched it but did not find the 'Secret Annexe'. After this fright, Anne wrote the following in her diary.

Who has inflicted this upon us? Who has made us Jews different from all other people? Who has allowed us to suffer so terribly up until now? ... If we bear all this suffering, and if there are still Jews left when it is over, then Jews, instead of being doomed, will be held up as an example ... During that night [of the search] I really felt I had to die; I waited for the police, I was prepared, as the soldier is on the battlefield, I was eager to lay down my life for my country ... Now I've been saved again, my first wish after the war is that I may become Dutch! ... I love the Dutch, I love this country, I love the language and want to work here.

found the Annexe and gossiped about it within earshot of Dutch Nazis or Germans?

As months grew into years Peter and Anne fell in love; according to Anne they kissed for the first time on 16 April 1944. Anne spent her days reading and learning English, French, geography, history and shorthand. She and her father amused themselves by writing poems to each other on important occasions. Sometimes they all entertained themselves by thinking of the first thing they would do when they were free. Margot and Mr Van Daan each wanted to wallow in a bath filled to the brim with hot water. Mrs Van Daan wanted to eat lots of cream cakes, Peter to go to the cinema, Anne 'to sit on a school bench' once again and continue her education (Source 17).

SOURCE 16

A page from Anne Frank's diary.

SOURCE 17

After nearly two years cooped up in the house Anne wrote this on 3 May 1944.

I have often been downcast, but never in despair; I regard our hiding as a dangerous adventure, romantic and interesting at the same time. In my diary I treat all the hardships as amusing. I have made up my mind now to lead a different life from other girls, and, later on, from ordinary housewives ... I am young and strong and am living a great adventure; I am still in the midst of it and can't grumble the whole day long ... Every day I feel ... that the liberation (freedom from Nazi rule) is drawing near and how beautiful nature is [and] how good the people are about me.

On 4 August 1944 Dutch informants led the Germans to the hideout. All those inside were arrested and sent to Auschwitz. Only Anne's father, Otto Frank, survived, rescued by the Red Army. Mr Van Daan is known to have been gassed. Anne's mother died in January 1945. Peter was moved out of Auschwitz with thousands of others when the Russians drew near. He was never heard of again. Anne and Margot died of typhus in Belsen in March 1945. When Otto Frank returned to the Netherlands he found Anne's diary had been kept by friends. He arranged to have it published. 'It would be quite funny ten years after the war if we Jews were to tell ... how we lived', Anne had written. Today, millions who never knew Anne Frank know her story.

The Nuremberg trial

When the death camps were opened there was a world-wide outcry. It was decided that people guilty of such 'crimes against humanity' must be punished. The trial of 22 leading Nazis began on 20 November 1945 at Nuremberg in Germany. The charges against them ranged from 'waging aggressive war', using slave labour, torturing and killing prisoners of war, to the mass murder of the Jews.

Some of the most guilty could not be brought to trial. Hitler was already dead. Goebbels and Himmler had also committed suicide. Another leading Nazi, Martin Bormann, Hitler's secretary, had disappeared and was never found. The most important Nazi leader in the dock at Nuremberg was Hermann Goering, Hitler's right-hand man since the Nazi movement's earliest days. Joachim von Ribbentrop, Nazi Foreign Minister, and two generals were also tried.

The trial, which lasted nine months, was often dull even though powerful emotions were never far from the surface (**Source 18**). Day after day lawyers, witnesses and the accused men argued over millions of words of evidence (**Source 19**). Once the court was shown film of the concentration

QUESTIONS

1 Give two reasons why Hitler's opponents were slow to react to Vrba and Wetzler's report (Source 9).

2 To have been freed by the Allies, roughly how much longer would Anne Frank and her family have needed to hide? (Look back to Chapter 5.)

3 Can you think of reasons why only Germans were tried for war crimes at Nuremberg?

4 Norman Birkett (Source 19) is attempting to answer critics of the Nuremberg trial. Can you work out what some of the criticisms were?

SOURCE 18

This incident at Nuremberg was reported in the *Daily Herald* newspaper on 4 March 1947.

The Russian prosecutor's voice droned on. He was speaking about the murder of millions of men, women and children. The court yawned ... We were thankful when the court rose and we filed out to the ... cafeteria ... Presently a Russian captain entered. We saw him pay ... for his snack and put down his tray. Suddenly he plunged his head in his hands and began to sob, 'Oh mother, sweet mother, dear father, why did they kill you?' ... With understanding in our hearts we went back to the court.

SOURCE 19

Norman Birkett, a British prosecuting lawyer, had this to say about the Nuremberg trial.

The thing which sustains me is the knowledge that this trial can be a very great landmark in ... international law ... Aggressor nations, great and small, will embark on war with the certain knowledge that if they fail they will be called to grim account. To make the trial secure against all criticism it must be shown to be fair, convincing and built on evidence that cannot be shaken as the years go past. That is why the trial is taking so much time and why documents are being piled on documents.

camps. Glimpses of the horrors – piles of shrunken bodies, men and women being burned alive, even a lampshade made from tattooed human flesh – horrified everybody in the court. Some of the prisoners looked away or covered their eyes. Even the arrogant Goering seemed shaken.

The accused men could say little in their defence, except that they did not know about the camps, or had merely been obeying orders. They denied that they had planned an aggressive war. Nineteen were found guilty. Some were given long terms of imprisonment. Eleven of the guilty were sentenced to death. Ten were executed on 17 October 1946; Goering cheated the US army hangman by taking poison.

SOURCE 20

The accused Nazis in the dock at Nuremberg. Goering is on the extreme left, resting his arm on the dock. Next to him is Rudolf Hess, Hitler's deputy, who flew to England in May 1941 to try to make peace between Britain and Germany. Joachim von Ribbentrop, the Nazi Foreign Minister, who went to Moscow in August 1939 to sign the Nazi – Soviet Pact, is on Hess's left.

Assessment tasks

A Knowledge and understanding

1 'The people of Poland suffered terribly and some of the war's most evil deeds occurred on Polish soil.'
   a Make a timeline of happenings between 1939 and 1945 which supports this statement. Include not just events in particular years but also things that happened over a longer period.
   b Why was Poland in a particularly exposed position during the Second World War?

2 a What were Hitler's reasons for killing Jews?
   b Which reason do you think was the most important to Hitler, and why?

3 Can you explain why many ordinary people on both sides in the war either took part in acts of mass murder or accepted such acts without protest?

B Interpretations and sources

4 Here are some later views of the Nuremberg trial.

   Some of the convictions [at Nuremberg] were for true war crimes – mass murder and the killing of prisoners of war. The tribunal (court) also devised the crime of preparing or waging aggressive war, which meant in practice war against ... the Allies ... The German leaders, especially the generals, could assert (claim) that they were really convicted for the crime of having lost.
   (A.J.P. Taylor, 1965)

   The Nuremberg trials were badly conducted and became a travesty (distortion) of justice. The accusers were also the judges. The Russians claimed that the Nazis were guilty of the Katyn massacre ... although the judges must have known that the Russians committed this crime ... In spite of being accused of plotting an aggressive war, the defendants were not allowed to point out that the Russians had committed unprovoked aggression not only in Poland but also in Finland.
   (Richard Lamb, 1993)

   The trial was much more than a hearing of cases against twenty-odd men accused of crimes against the law of war and against humanity ... Many people saw it as ... a vital experiment in international co-operation and the application of law ... It was part of the search for a better way to control strong human impulses, aggression and revenge. It was an attempt to replace violence with acceptable and effective rules for human behaviour.
   (Ann and John Tusa, 1983)

   a What are the main differences between these accounts?
   b Are the differences based upon historical evidence, the opinions of the writers, or both?
   c Which account do you find the most convincing, and why?

5 Compare Sources 2, 15 and 17. How useful are they in helping us to understand what it was like to live under threat of murder?

6 Re-read Sources 4 and 9.
   a What reasons could there be for either (i) doubting, or (ii) trusting, their reliability?
   b In your opinion, how reliable and valuable are these sources?

9 The Cold War and Post-War Problems

Russia, the UN, Israel and Korea

In 1946 Winston Churchill was invited to Fulton College, Missouri, in the United States, to give a speech to staff and students. Missouri was President Truman's home state. When Truman was shown the invitation he scribbled on the bottom, 'Dear Winnie. This is a fine old school ... If you come and make a speech there I'll take you out and introduce you'. So when Churchill rose to speak, on 5 March, the President was on the platform with him.

One sentence in Churchill's speech had a dramatic effect. Speaking of post-war Europe, he said, 'From Stettin in the Baltic to Trieste in the Adriatic, an iron curtain has descended across the continent'. The words 'iron curtain' hit world headlines the next day. They have become a catchphrase through the years. But what was the 'Iron Curtain' and why did Churchill warn his audience about it?

Soviet takeovers

Russia ended the war with enlarged boundaries and an extra 22 million people taken from parts of Germany, Poland and Czechoslovakia. During the Red Army's

SOURCE 1

Winston Churchill about to make his famous 'Iron Curtain' speech at Fulton, Missouri, on 5 March 1946. President Truman is standing behind him.

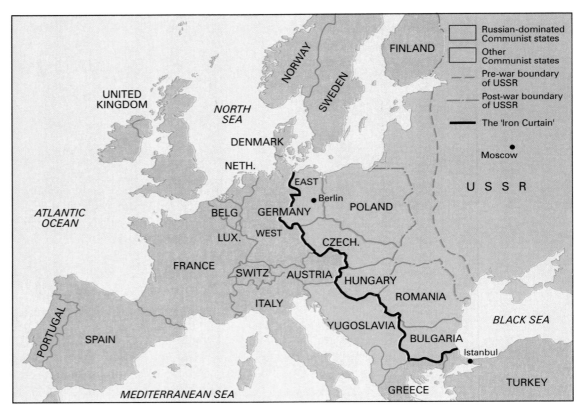

Post-war Europe and the Iron Curtain

Winston Churchill included Yugoslavia in his definition of the 'Iron Curtain', but although the country had a Communist government it remained independent of the USSR.

advance in 1944–5, Hungary, Bulgaria, Czechoslovakia, Romania and Poland had been occupied. Yet such conquests had been gained at a terrible cost. Twenty million Russians had died in the war; 50 for every one American killed. Thousands of cities, towns and villages lay in ruins. Much of the Soviet railway system was out of action. The countryside was devastated and neglected.

A future British Prime Minister, Anthony Eden, had this to say about the Soviet attitude after the war in a speech on 26 February 1946.

It is difficult for us to understand the profound (deep) impression ... made upon the minds of the Soviet government and people by the wide and deep invasion of their land by ... German armies and ... the [resulting] distress and suffering ... It is difficult for an island people (the British) to entirely understand it ... I am convinced that the fear of invasion ... is the dominant motive in Soviet foreign policy ... [The Russians] are determined that Germany shall not be in a position to [invade] again ... [and] to have as friendly neighbours as they can.

In such circumstances Stalin had two main aims. First, he needed to rebuild Soviet industry, chiefly by making the Germans pay reparations (compensation) for the damage their armies had done. Second, to lessen the chances of another invasion, he wanted to make sure Russia had friendly countries on its western borders **(Source 2)**. Both aims brought him into conflict with his wartime allies, particularly the USA and Britain. The Americans and British were against reparations and agreed to them only reluctantly. Later, they were appalled by the wholesale stripping of German industry in the Soviet-occupied regions and its transportation to Russia **(Source 3)**.

Stalin's other aim – to achieve secure borders – brought more serious conflict. The only way the Soviet dictator could be sure of friendly neighbours was to set up Communist governments in eastern Europe. As early as 1944 he had established Communist rule in Poland. This meant that a war begun to save the Poles from a Nazi dictator had ended with them in the grip of a

Communist one! Once the fighting was over, Stalin set about turning neighbouring countries Communist. One by one, Bulgaria, Romania, Czechoslovakia and Hungary fell to Communist trickery and violence. The peoples of these countries were given no choice but to live under Stalin's terror.

These takeovers, which Stalin claimed were triumphs of the working classes over their masters, ended with the collapse of democratic government in Czechoslovakia in 1948 (**Source 4**). The Iron Curtain of which Churchill had spoken two years before was complete. It was the dividing line between Communist and democratic Europe.

Communism versus capitalism

The quarrels between Russia and its wartime allies never led to open warfare. Russia had atomic weapons by 1949 so the fear of nuclear war made sure of that. Nevertheless the disputes were so bitter that they became known as the *cold war*. They were made worse because Russia was Communist and the West capitalist. To the Americans, the situation was even more dangerous because many westerners found Communist ideas attractive. Most western

SOURCE 4

Here an eyewitness describes the arrival of the Red Army in Czechoslovakia in 1948.

First the tank divisions, well disciplined, well armed and trained ... the columns of guns and lorries, the parachute divisions, motor cyclists, technical units, then columns of marching soldiers, dirty, tired, clad in ragged uniforms ... then women and girls in military uniforms, high boots and tight blouses, with long hair greased with goosefat. Then ... lorries belonging to the political staff and motorised units of the political police, then lorries with tonnes of caviar, sturgeon, salami ... vodka and wine ... And finally the rearguard: miles and miles of small light carts drawn by Cossack horses ... a flood ... spreading across Europe.

states had Communist parties. They were particularly powerful in France and Italy, where they had spearheaded the wartime resistance to Nazi rule. Western leaders were afraid that such groups might gain power, either legally or by force, and destroy democracy.

If the West feared Communism, many Communists feared capitalism. Communists claimed that the trade competition between nations encouraged by capitalism often led to war. Furthermore, they maintained that in times of trade depression capitalist governments reduced unemployment by increasing weapons production. So capitalism, in their opinion, was by its very nature a threat to world peace. In February 1946 Stalin referred to this in a broadcast. He warned his people that the United States was likely to attack Russia, and used this threat as an excuse to start another Five Year Plan of rearmament.

With each side afraid of the other, relations quickly worsened between the two power blocs (groups). In 1947 President Truman decided that Soviet expansion must be stopped. He offered to send aid to any country threatened by a Communist takeover (**Source 5**). This 'Truman Doctrine' was first used to help Greece and Turkey; in Greece it led to the defeat of the Communists in a civil war. American aid to Europe was extended under the Marshall Plan, named after the US general who supervised it. This was a scheme of financial and material help to assist Europe's recovery from the devastation of war.

Marshall claimed that his plan would fight 'hunger, poverty, desperation and chaos' in countries hard-hit by the war. Stalin thought it was a way of increasing American domination of European states by controlling their industry and finance (**Source 7**). He refused to accept Marshall Aid for Russia or its allies. Consequently from 1947 the recovery of western Europe was accelerated while the standard of living in the east remained low.

QUESTIONS

1. Why did Anthony Eden think 'an island people' would find it hard to understand Russian feelings after the war (Source 2)?

2. What does Source 4 tell you about life in the Red Army?

3. Why did the USA become so heavily involved in Europe after the war?

4. What factors led people in western Germany to be much better off than those in eastern Germany in the post-war years?

SOURCE 5

Speaking to the US Congress in March 1947, President Truman gave his reasons for offering help against Communist aggression.

At the present moment in world history nearly every nation must choose between alternative ways of life. The choice is too often not a free one. One way ... is based upon the will of the majority ... [with] representative government, individual liberty, freedom of speech and religion ... The second way of life is based upon the will of the minority forcibly imposed upon the majority. It relies upon terror and oppression, a controlled press and radio, fixed elections ... I believe that we must assist free peoples to work out their own destinies ... through ... financial aid.

SOURCE 6

This is how an American cartoonist imagined Stalin's reaction to the Truman Doctrine. The Soviet dictator was a keen pipe-smoker.

SOURCE 7

Andrei Vyshinsky, Soviet Deputy Foreign Minister, stated the Russian view of the Truman Doctrine at the United Nations in September 1947.

The so-called Truman Doctrine and Marshall Plan are ... glaring examples of the manner in which the principles of the United Nations are violated ... The United States [has] attempted to impose its will on other independent states ... using resources distributed ... to needy nations as an instrument of political pressure ... The Marshall Plan will mean placing European countries under the ... control of the United States [with] direct interference in the internal affairs of those countries.

The German problem

The defeat of Germany left a large, conquered territory in the centre of Europe, divided into military zones by the British, Americans, Russians and French. Clearly, this was an unsatisfactory situation which could not last. Both Russia and the western countries agreed that Germany must be united again under an effective government. However, each wanted it united on their own terms. For Stalin, this meant a Communist Germany; for the Allies, a capitalist one. Since neither could agree to the other's plan, Germany remained divided.

Stalin was sure that a capitalist Germany, supported by the West, would attack Russia again within 15 years. To prevent this happening he continued to strip German industry in the Soviet zone and carry off machines and equipment to Russia. The British and Americans thought this policy was not only wrong but also dangerous. If the Germans were badly treated and again left with a grievance, as they had been after the First World War, permanent peace would be at risk. They warned the Soviet leader that his policies towards Germany might lead to the rise of another Hitler. Stalin did not agree. He believed that the West was 'too soft' with the Germans, pointing out that Russia had been devastated by Nazi armies while the United States had not been damaged at all.

In January 1947 the American and British zones of Germany were joined. Stalin saw this as a move towards creating a separate West Germany dominated by the USA. He struck back at what he thought was the Allies' weakest spot – Berlin. Although the German capital was inside the Russian zone, it, too, was split into sectors run by the British, Americans, Russians and French. In June 1948 the Russians closed all road, rail and canal links between Berlin and the western zones, and cut off food, electricity and gas supplies to the Allied sectors of the city.

Stalin hoped this blockade would force

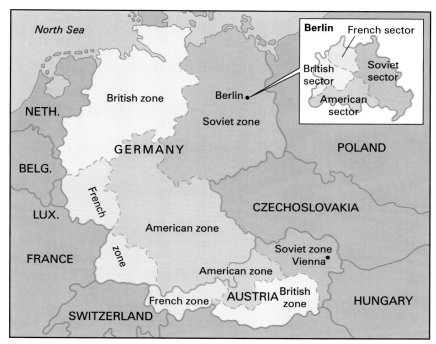

Germany divided in defeat

Like Germany, Austria was occupied by the victorious Allies and divided into administrative zones.

the Allies to give up their plans for a separate West Germany. In fact, his action had the opposite effect. The Allies decided to supply the two million people in their sectors of Berlin by airlift **(Source 8)**. For ten months pilots flew in all weathers to keep the inhabitants of the Allied sectors supplied with essentials; at one time a transport plane was landing every five minutes. That winter the citizens walked miles to work, shared fires and food and lived by candlelight. They accepted these hardships gladly rather than give in to the Russians. 'We'd rather go hungry than go Commie' was their slogan.

The Berlin blockade made the division of Germany certain. In April 1949 the French

joined the British and Americans in setting up the Federal Republic of Germany (West Germany). In May, Stalin admitted defeat and lifted the blockade. However, he soon turned the Russian zone into the German Democratic Republic (East Germany). That year the Allies formed the North Atlantic Treaty Organisation (NATO) to stop further Russian expansion. The Communist bloc formed a similar grouping in eastern Europe in 1955 called the Warsaw Pact.

The United Nations

In 1945 representatives of 50 nations met in San Francisco, USA, and signed a United Nations Charter. This replaced the covenant (constitution) of the League of Nations. The old League had failed to keep world peace. Many large countries, notably the United States, had never joined, and it had never had an army to enforce its decisions. At San Francisco, all the victorious nations, as well as many which had remained neutral during the war, joined the new organisation.

Furthermore, the new Charter allowed for member states to provide armed forces to deal with aggression or keep the peace in trouble spots.

The General Assembly of the United Nations Organisation (UNO) meets in New York. Each member state can send up to five representatives, although they have only one vote. A Secretary-General is in charge of the day to day running of the UN. This person is chosen from a small country; the first was Trygve-Lie, a Norwegian **(Source 11)**. In addition, the Security Council meets regularly to deal with urgent problems. Britain, France, the USA, Russia and China have permanent seats on this council. The remaining places are taken by other states in rotation. Security Council decisions must be passed by at least seven of the eleven members, including all of the 'Big Five'. This gives the permanent members the right to veto (reject) any proposal. Until 1950, when the rules were changed, Russia used the veto frequently during its disputes with the West.

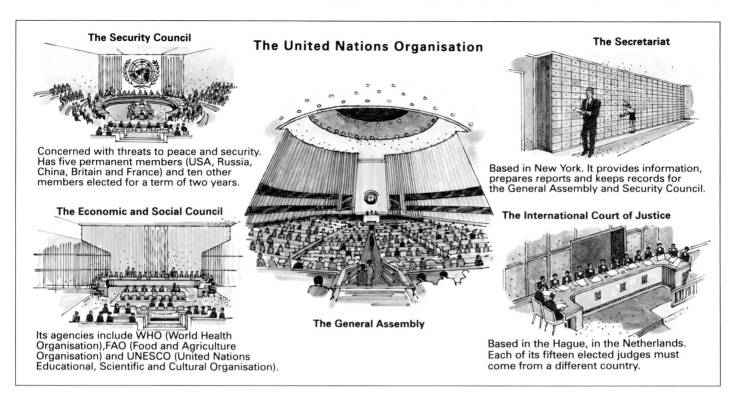

The United Nations Organisation

The Security Council

Concerned with threats to peace and security. Has five permanent members (USA, Russia, China, Britain and France) and ten other members elected for a term of two years.

The Secretariat

Based in New York. It provides information, prepares reports and keeps records for the General Assembly and Security Council.

The Economic and Social Council

Its agencies include WHO (World Health Organisation),FAO (Food and Agriculture Organisation) and UNESCO (United Nations Educational, Scientific and Cultural Organisation).

The General Assembly

The International Court of Justice

Based in the Hague, in the Netherlands. Each of its fifteen elected judges must come from a different country.

Besides keeping the peace, the UN employs special agencies to do important work. Some, like the International Court of Justice, were part of the old League of Nations. Others were set up by UNO. The World Health Organisation (WHO) combats disease throughout the world, helping with medical research and training doctors and nurses. The Food and Agriculture Organisation (FAO) deals with pest control, irrigation and improved farming techniques – matters of life and death in many parts of the world. Since 1951, FAO experts have helped the peoples of poorer countries to improve their farming, fishing and forestry.

The United Nations aims to feed minds as well as bodies. The UN Educational, Scientific and Cultural Organisation (UNESCO) tries to increase knowledge and foster goodwill and understanding among peoples. It publishes books, organises exhibitions and conferences, and sets up schools, colleges and universities where they are most needed. The UN International Children's Emergency Fund (UNICEF) is supported entirely by voluntary donations. It supplies everything from food and medicines to machinery and bicycles to help the poor and underprivileged.

SOURCE 11

Dag Hammarskjöld, a Swede, was the second UN Secretary-General. He was killed in an air crash in 1961 while on a peace mission to Africa. He had this to say of the UN's importance.

It is not the Soviet Union, nor indeed any great powers, who need the United Nations, for they have protection. It is all the others. In this sense, the United Nations is first of all their organisation. And I deeply believe in the wisdom with which they will be able to use it and guide it.

SOURCE 10

The General Assembly of the United Nations in session at the UN headquarters in New York.

In 1948 members of the UN issued a Universal Declaration of Human Rights, pledging themselves to work for what Roosevelt had called 'the four freedoms' – freedom from want and fear and freedom of speech and worship. Altogether, the Declaration lists 30 essential rights and freedoms **(Source 12)**. Much of the UN's work has been to deal with denials of such rights, and breakdowns of the peace, in various parts of the world.

The UN in Palestine – the birth of Israel

In Palestine, Arabs and Jews had long been in conflict. Originally it had been a home for both Arab and Jew, but the Jews had been driven out in ancient times. Jewish settlers from Europe began to return to Palestine at the end of the nineteenth century. They and their supporters in Europe started to work towards the creation of a permanent Jewish homeland in Palestine. They called themselves Zionists, after Zion, a hill in Jerusalem where Jews had once worshipped.

The Zionist dream was an Arab nightmare. Arabs saw it as an encouragement to outsiders to come and take their land. In the 1930s large numbers of German Jews arrived in Palestine, escaping from the Nazis. The Arabs felt threatened and reacted violently. Just before the Second World War the British, who then ruled Palestine, suggested dividing the country between the two communities. This was rejected by the Arabs **(Source 13)**. After the war the situation grew worse. Thousands more Jews, many of them survivors of the death camps, came to Palestine. This led to open warfare between Arabs and Jews. Unwilling to continue policing the country, the British pulled out in 1948 after handing over the problem to the United Nations.

The UN produced another plan to divide Palestine. Again, this was rejected by the Arabs. On the day British rule ended, Zionists took matters into their own hands and set up the state of Israel. In the war

SOURCE 12

Here are some of the most important Articles of the Universal Declaration of Human Rights.

All human beings are born free and equal. Everyone has the right to life, liberty and personal security.
No one shall be made a slave ... be tortured or suffer cruel punishment.
No one shall be arrested without a reason, or imprisoned without a trial.
Everyone has the right to think and say what they like, to practise their religion freely and ... to come together in peaceful assembly.
Everyone has the right to take part in the government of their country, either directly or through freely chosen representatives.
Everyone has the right to work, to free choice of employment ... to join a trade union ... to be educated ... to have housing and medical care and necessary social services.

SOURCE 13

In 1946 a British politician asked an Arab leader why the Palestinians could not accept the Jews as brothers. This was his reply.

Our brother [the Jew] has gone to Europe and the West and come back something else. He has come back a Russified Jew, a Polish Jew, a German Jew, an English Jew. He has come back with a totally different outlook on things, western not eastern. That does not mean we are ... necessarily quarrelling with anyone who comes from the West. But ... the Zionist, the new Jew, wants to dominate ... His excuse [is] that the Arab people are backward and he has got a mission to put them forward ... the Arabs simply stand and say 'No'.

The creation of Israel

Jewish refugees arrive in Palestine in April 1947. The British authorities there tried to stop such ships landing. This led Jewish gunmen to attack British troops in Palestine.

which followed the Palestinian Arabs were assisted by the Arab states of Syria, Iraq, Egypt, Jordan and Lebanon. Even so, they were heavily defeated and driven from their homes. By October 1948 the Israelis had seized more territory than the UN plan had allowed them. Palestinian refugees settled in neighbouring Arab countries in makeshift camps **(Source 15)**. The UN managed to negotiate a ceasefire but not before one of its representatives, Count Bernadotte, had been murdered by Jews. Since that time three wars between Israel and the Arabs have led to more Arab defeats and more seizure of territory by Israelis.

SOURCE 15

This is part of a Jewish writer's description of Israel in 1949, just after the first Arab-Israeli war ended.

In Jerusalem [and many other towns] Arabs owned many modern houses. As a result of the great onrush of Jewish immigrants during the last nine months, all these houses have been taken over [by Jews] ... The slum sections of most cities have either been destroyed by warfare or dynamited in order to clear the way for proper city planning ... In other words, there is not a house in the cities of Israel which is free to accommodate its pre-war owners [the Arabs]. The same is true of the bigger and more prosperous villages.

SOURCE 16

United Nations relief workers distributing milk to Arabs at a refugee camp outside the Israeli border (1949).

QUESTIONS

1 What did the permanent members of the UN Security Council have in common? What divided them?

2 Explain the link between Nazi rule in Germany and the setting up of the state of Israel in 1948.

3 How did the actions of Russia and America contribute to (a) the start of the war in Korea, and (b) the United Nations' involvement in the war?

4 Why did Russia's seizure of Czechoslovakia after the war bring back what Oliver Franks called 'ghastly memories' of 1938 (Source 17)?

The Korean war

The UN fights a war in Korea

Korea is a peninsula to the south-east of Manchuria which was conquered by the Japanese in 1910. When the Pacific war ended in 1945, both Russian and American troops moved in. A temporary dividing line between the two armies became fixed when the Russians set up a Communist state in the north, and the Americans a capitalist one in the south.

In January 1950 the United States listed those countries in South-East Asia it was prepared to defend against Communist aggression. These did not include Korea. In June, North Korea, backed by Russia, invaded the south in a bid to unite the country by force. They did not expect any US interference. But the attack came at a time when Russia had walked out of the UN Security Council because the US would not let the new Communist government of China join the United Nations. Without a Russian veto to stop them, the Americans were able to persuade the General Assembly to send troops to defend South Korea **(Source 17)**. Only five years after its foundation, the UN was drawn into war.

SOURCE 17

Oliver Franks was on a British government mission to the United States at the time of the outbreak of the Korean War. Here he gives his opinion of why the Americans decided to intervene.

These (the seizure of Czechoslovakia, the Berlin blockade and the invasion of South Korea) were seen as stages in Soviet risk-taking which would culminate (end) with their armed forces crossing boundaries. It is hard now to remember the shudder about the Russian seizure of Czechoslovakia, and the ghastly memories that it evoked of 1938 (the Munich Crisis) ... There was a sense of not knowing where the Russians would break out next ... I favoured countering the North Korean invasion because I thought that if any army could cross any frontier when it chose, then chaos had come.

These soldiers from Australia and New Zealand were part of the United Nations force sent to fight in the Korean War.

The shock caused by the Chinese attack is shown in this letter from an American soldier, James Cardinal, to his parents, 7 January 1951.

We are now about 60 miles north-west of Taegu, holding a mountain pass through which the entire (US) 8th Army is moving heading south. It looks like the beginning of the end. The Chinese are kicking hell out of the US army, and I think we are getting out, at least I hope so ... It's impossible to stop these Chinese hordes. There's just too many of them for us to fight in Korea ... We all feel we've been let down by our ... blundering leadership ... If we must fight Communism, let's do it in Europe ... [not] some barren oriental wasteland.

Although fifteen countries, including Britain, sent troops, the UN forces were chiefly American; the USA had a large army and navy based in nearby Japan. Taken by surprise, the North Koreans were driven out. In October 1950 the UN army captured Pyongyang, the North Korean capital. This brought them close to the Chinese border. Mao Zedong, China's Communist leader, decided that his country was in danger and sent his army across the frontier. Mass attacks by 300,000 Chinese troops drove the Americans back in disorderly retreat and it was some time before the UN could be sure of even holding on in the south **(Source 19)**. It took three years of hard fighting before the Chinese agreed to leave and a truce between the two sides was signed at Panmunjom (1953). Prompt action by the UN had saved South Korea. But it had not brought permanent peace after a war costing nearly two million lives.

Assessment tasks

A Knowledge and understanding

1 What factors helped the countries of western Europe to recover from the war more quickly than the 'Iron Curtain' countries in the east?

2 a List the main aims of the United Nations Organisation under the following headings: (i) *political* (to do with those who have power and the way decisions are made), (ii) *economic* (to do with creating and distributing wealth), and (iii) *social* (things affecting people's way of life).
  b Summarise the differences between the United Nations and the former League of Nations.

3 The 1948 United Nations declaration of universal human rights was just wishful thinking ... Rights only exist as part of the traditions and beliefs of a society : outside rich and developed countries they mostly do not. Solemn post-war declarations about ... everyone's right to freedom and a fair trial are and always were empty ... The UN has neither the will nor the power to implement them.
(Minette Marrin, 1993)

  a What do you think the writer means by 'rich and developed countries'? Give some examples.
  b In 1948 it was only in countries of this kind that many of the human rights proclaimed in the Declaration were to be found. What does this suggest about the United Nations as an organisation?
  c Can the Declaration serve any useful purpose if the United Nations is unable to enforce it?

B Interpretations and sources

4 Here are two views of the creation of the state of Israel in 1948.

Palestine was [once] recognised universally as 'the land of the Jews'. From the sixteenth century onward, the land had been under non-Arab (mainly Turkish) rule... [The Holocaust led] homeless survivors to emigrate to Palestine, the land of the Jews... It was, they reasoned, because they had no land of their own that six million of them had been inhumanly slaughtered ... They were too tired to attempt a new life in a place where, some day, someone might cry, 'Jews get out!' ... In Palestine a National Home was eager to receive them.
(Abba Eban, 1969)

Israel came into existence as a result of ... atrocious crimes perpetrated against European Jewry in sight of Europe and the world; and as a result of the exertions of leading Jews who worked ... to capture a piece of territory not their own ... That the Jews had suffered at the hands of Christian Europeans through the ages seemed a poor reason for allowing them to expropriate (take over) a part of the Arab world and drive a million Muslims out of it.
(Peter Calvocoressi, 1968)

  a What are the points of agreement and disagreement between the two accounts?
  b What do these tell you about each writer's views?

5 Compare Sources 5 and 7.
  a How does each reflect the political bias of the speaker?
  b Explain how sources of this kind can be unreliable yet at the same time provide useful historical evidence.

6 a What different views about the threat of Communism are revealed in Sources 17 and 19?
  b How might these views reflect the situation each man finds himself in?

Britain, the Empire and Europe

On 5 July 1945 Britain went to the polls to choose a new government. The Conservatives had won the last General Election in 1935. During the war the main political parties had joined in a coalition led by Winston Churchill, a Conservative. Counting the votes took three weeks because so many servicemen and women were abroad. The result was a sensational victory for the Labour party which won 393 seats in the House of Commons to the Conservatives' 213 and the Liberals' 12 **(Source 2)**. Churchill was out, replaced by Clement Attlee, the Labour leader. Attlee's first speech to the Commons as Prime Minister was to announce Japan's surrender.

SOURCE 1

Churchill with King George VI, Queen Elizabeth and the Princesses Elizabeth (left) and Margaret greet crowds from the balcony of Buckingham Palace on VE (Victory in Europe) Day, 8 May 1945. Two months later Churchill was voted out of office.

SOURCE 2

A Labour supporter remembers 26 July 1945 – the day the General Election results came through.

I will always remember 26th July as a sunny day – I don't know whether it was. My friends and I had not expected to win. We remembered 1935 ... We thought the Tories were too smart. They would always kid the masses. The young people did not know the 1930s. The old ones would thank Churchill for a good war. My heart was in my mouth with every result. I thought I was dreaming.

SOURCE 3

Clement Attlee, Labour Prime Minister 1945-51, pictured in July 1945. In his broadcast on VJ (Victory over Japan) Day, 15 August 1945, he did not mention Churchill.

A new start with Labour

Opinion polls predicted a Labour success but they had been largely ignored as 'new fangled' and unreliable. How could Churchill, the great wartime leader, be rejected by the voters at the moment of victory **(Source 4)**? Foreigners, in particular, were amazed. But there were good reasons for the upset. Churchill, although a Conservative, had been against the pre-war appeasement policy of his own government, believing it encouraged Hitler's aggression and made war unavoidable. By 1945 millions of British people agreed with him. But whatever pride and gratitude they felt for Churchill the war-leader, a majority were firmly against the Conservative party.

If voters remembered the past in 1945, they also looked to the future. For six years they had been united as never before, sharing dangers, hardships, rationing and restrictions, regardless of class or income. Times had been hard and everywhere Britain showed the signs of war **(Source 5).** With the coming of peace the people wanted to share in the rewards of victory; in particular they expected better housing, education, health care and welfare benefits.

In 1942 the 'brave new world' which the Beveridge Report promised (see page 79) had been welcomed by all political parties. Churchill, however, had refused to do anything about the Report until the war was over. This was a mistake because it gave the impression that he was half-hearted about social reform. Churchill's aristocratic background – he was the cousin of a Duke – and lack of sympathy with working-class people had often made him unpopular. Most people felt that if there was to be a new start it would have to be with a party which really believed in changing society.

The Welfare State

In 1945 few doubted that the 'bad old days' of the 1930s, with their mass unemployment, poverty and inequality, must be banished for ever. Even before Labour came to power the coalition government had made a start with two important reforms.

SOURCE 4

On the day Japan surrendered there was a victory broadcast on the BBC. Winston Churchill was not invited to speak, to the displeasure of the writer of this letter to *The Times*.

Sir,
It has been stated that, on the day of victory, broadcasts will be given by both the King and the Prime Minister (Clement Attlee). May we be bold enough to ask for a broadcast from the Leader of the Opposition (Churchill)? Whatever the mistakes of a party which has consequently been swept out of power, Mr Winston Churchill cannot but remain the man who led this Empire's part in the final overthrowing of Japan. There is no other man more ... qualified to speak in celebration of this occasion.

G. Spencer Brown, Priors Mount, Gt. Malvern.

In August 1945 J.L. Hodson, a journalist, described a journey in post-war Britain.

The war is over; the conditions of war in some respects continue. You need only make a long railway journey in England to become aware of it. I travelled last Sunday to Newcastle upon Tyne. The journey which in peacetime took four hours now took eight and a quarter. No food on the train. No cup of tea to be got at the stops because the queues ... were impossibly long. At Newcastle ... no taxi to be got. My hotel towel is about the size of a pocket handkerchief; the soap tablet is worn to the thinness of paper; my bed sheets are torn.

In 1944 Parliament passed an Education Act which set the pattern for schooling in England and Wales after the war. Elementary schools, where many working-class children spent their whole school life until they left at fourteen, were to be abolished. In future, both primary *and* secondary education would be provided free for every child. The school leaving age was to be raised to fifteen almost immediately (this was eventually done in 1947) and later to sixteen. Children with disabilities were to be properly catered for. Local Education Authorities were required to provide suitable schools for all children, according to 'age, aptitude and ability' – and milk, meals and medical and dental services as well.

A scheme of Family Allowances (later called Child Benefit) was also introduced by the wartime coalition government. These allowances, originally set at 5 shillings (25p) per week for each child in the family except the first-born, channelled extra income into

QUESTIONS

1. Why would foreigners have found it particularly hard to understand Churchill's election defeat in 1945?

2. Although the Conservatives welcomed the Beveridge Report in 1942, how might it have contributed to their election defeat three years later?

3. In Source 7 the Conservatives appear to be claiming a share of the credit for the Labour government's National Insurance scheme. What could be the reason for this?

4. Does the *Daily Mail* seem to approve wholeheartedly of the Welfare State (Source 9), or can you find reservations in its report?

SOURCE 6

One of the new schools resulting from the 1944 Education Act – Smallberry Green Secondary Modern School for Boys, Isleworth, Middlesex, opened in 1947.

families at the time when it was most needed. The money was paid to the mother as it was felt that she would be more likely to spend it on the children.

After 1945 the pace of reform quickened. To make up for homes lost in the air-raids, the Government began a massive programme of building council houses for renting. At the same time new towns were established around London and other large cities to reduce overcrowding in the main centres of population. In line with the Beveridge Report, the Government extended National Insurance to every person of working age (except married women, for whom the scheme was optional). In return for weekly contributions, benefits were paid during times of sickness or unemployment and in old age **(Source 7)**. A National Assistance Board was also set up to provide a 'safety net' for disabled people and others whose needs were not met through the insurance scheme.

The Labour government's greatest achievement was to set up the National Health Service (NHS). This came into operation on 5 July 1948 – the so-called 'Appointed Day' when the main services of Britain's new Welfare State began **(Source 9)**. The whole range of medical treatment, including the services of dentists and opticians, was provided free to everyone. There was an immediate rush for treatment. 'One would think the people saved up their illnesses for the first free day', remarked one busy doctor. In a way

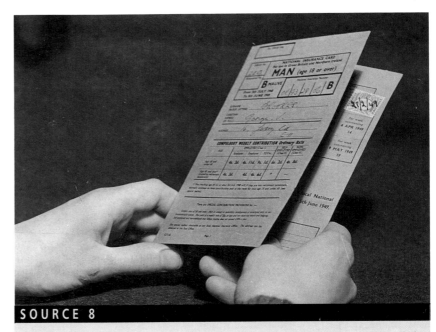

SOURCE 8

When the new National Insurance scheme started, in 1948, contributions were recorded by sticking special stamps on cards like the one pictured here. People were given a number because so many had the same name. In 1948 there were 650,000 Smiths, including 8000 John Smiths!

SOURCE 9

On 3 July 1948, the *Daily Mail* said this to its readers about the beginning of Britain's Welfare State.

On Monday morning you will wake in a new Britain, in a state which 'takes over' its citizens six months before they are born, providing care and free services for their birth, for their early years, their schooling, sickness, workless days, widowhood and retirement. All this, with free doctoring, dentistry and medicine – free bath-chairs, too, if needed – for 4s 11d (25p) out of your weekly pay packet. You begin paying next Friday.

SOURCE 7

Speaking for the Conservatives in the House of Commons, R.A. Butler said this of Labour's National Insurance scheme.

I think we should take pride that the British race has been able ... shortly after the terrible period through which we have all passed together, to show the whole world that we are able to produce a social insurance scheme of this character.

this was true. Before the NHS, many people who were sick, or who suffered with bad teeth or poor eyesight, went without treatment because they could not afford it. So it was hardly surprising that dentists who in the past had rarely seen poor patients unless they were in agony with toothache now had waiting lists. Similarly, poor people who needed to wear glasses could now get a proper pair from an optician and throw away the sixpenny pair they had bought at Woolworths!

SOURCE 10

A crowded doctor's waiting room in London shortly after the start of the National Health Service. For the first time medical care was free to all.

From Empire to Commonwealth

An African soldier returning to a British colony after the war remarked, 'We overseas soldiers are coming home with new ideas'. Chief among these new ideas was a desire for independence. The war had increased the chances of success for such demands. Most countries with colonies – Britain, Italy, Belgium, Holland and France – had been weakened by the war. Some had suffered defeat and occupation. Britain was deeply in debt and needed a large American loan to assist its recovery. It could not afford to hold down discontented territories for long. In any case, it was the policy of Britain's new Labour government to dismantle the empire.

Independence was among the freedoms promised in the Atlantic Charter (see page 43). To some, this had only meant freedom from the rule of dictators such as Hitler; Churchill, for instance, was proud of the British empire and against giving it up. But it was difficult for countries which had just fought a war for freedom to refuse to give it to their colonies. Moreover the two superpowers, Russia and the United States, were against colonial rule. Throughout the war, Roosevelt in particular had put pressure on Britain to give up its empire.

For the Labour government the first step was to leave India, Britain's most heavily populated possession **(Source 11)**. British rule, developed over 200 years, had brought its benefits to India but had never stopped Indians wanting self-government. To give them less cause for complaint, the British had granted the Indians a share in governing themselves. But Britain still had

SOURCE 11

A young Indian recalls the moment, sitting near a broken-down train in India, when he heard of the Labour victory in the British General Election.

We sat there ... on this moonlit night and a radio was on. The news that the British Labour Party had won the election came. There were only two Indians and we didn't know each other – the rest were all British. We both got up and started dancing and embraced each other. These poor British ... were absolutely disgusted. They knew why we were celebrating – this meant that Britain would soon relinquish (give up control of) India.

the final say; in 1939 the British Viceroy (governor) of India had declared war on India's behalf without consulting a single Indian! This enraged many Indians and some refused to co-operate with Britain even when their country was threatened by the Japanese (see page 65). The Indian army nevertheless remained loyal to Britain and fought bravely in many parts of the world. In return, Indians were promised their freedom at some future date.

It was already clear by 1945 that Indian independence could not be long delayed. It was also clear that the changeover would not be straightforward. India was a vast country of many peoples, deeply divided by language, religion and culture. In particular, there was a great deal of ill-feeling between Hindus and Muslims. The Muslims were outnumbered three to one by Hindus. They felt sure that they would have little say in a self-governing India run by Hindus and so demanded a separate Muslim state, to be called Pakistan (meaning 'the land of the pure'). The Hindus were against this idea. As the dispute grew more bitter, terrible riots led to bloodshed in many parts of India.

SOURCE 12

Mohandas Gandhi, leader of the Indian Congress Party which ran a 'quit India' campaign against the British during and after the Second World War. Gandhi achieved his life's ambition when India gained its independence (1947) but was assassinated a few months later.

SOURCE 13

In the run-up to Indian independence, disputes between Muslims and Hindus led to riots and hundreds of deaths in Indian cities. Here we see police using tear-gas to disperse a crowd trying to burn down a Hindu temple in Calcutta (August 1946).

In February 1947, Prime Minister Attlee announced that British rule in India would end no later than 1 June 1948. He chose a new Viceroy, Lord Mountbatten, to supervise the changeover. Mountbatten soon came to the conclusion that unless independence was granted quickly the rioting would develop into civil war. He named 15 August 1947 as the date for British withdrawal **(Source 14)**. On that date India was partitioned (divided) to give the Muslims their separate state of Pakistan. In the weeks that followed four and a half million Hindus fled to India and six million Muslims to Pakistan. This mass migration led to fearful massacres as Muslims and Hindus clashed on roads and at railway stations.

It was impossible for Britain to keep the rest of its empire once India had gone. In 1948 Palestine, Burma and Ceylon (now Sri Lanka) became independent. During the next 20 years large parts of Africa, the British West Indian islands, Malaysia and the Mediterranean colonies of Cyprus and Malta became self-governing **(Source 15)**. Britain preserved links with most of these states by inviting them to join a 'Commonwealth of Nations'. The new Commonwealth was a partnership of equals, not a colonial empire.

The partition of India

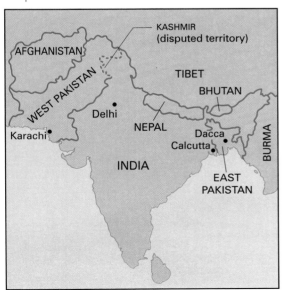

SOURCE 14

Lord Mountbatten's Chief-of-Staff, A. Campbell-Johnson, comments on the decision to speed up British withdrawal from India.

India in March 1947 was a ship on fire in mid-ocean with ammunition in the hold. By then it was a question of putting the fire out before it actually reached the ammunition. There was in fact no option before us but to do what we did.

SOURCE 15

This view of the ending of the British empire comes from Iain Macleod, a Conservative Secretary of State for the Colonies during the period of 'decolonisation'.

We could not possibly have held by force to our territories in Africa. We could not, with an enormous force engaged, even continue to hold the small island of Cyprus. General de Gaulle (President of France) could not contain Algeria. The march of men towards their freedom can be guided, but not halted. Of course there were risks in moving quickly. But the risks of moving slowly were far greater.

QUESTIONS

1. The Second World War has been described as 'the beginning of the end for the British empire'. Can you give reasons why?

2. Why was India like 'a ship on fire' in 1947 (Source 14)? What was the 'ammunition' in the hold?

3. Pakistan originally consisted of two parts – East and West Pakistan. Find out what happened to East Pakistan.

4. In Source 15 what kind of 'risks' might Iain Macleod have had in mind as a result of (a) moving quickly, and (b) moving slowly?

The new Europe

Nowhere was more in need of a fresh start in 1945 than Europe. Large areas of the continent were in ruins. Millions had been killed, and millions more were homeless or close to starving. It was time to replace the hatreds and rivalries of the past with goodwill and co-operation.

The basis of any lasting peace in Europe had to be close co-operation between

SOURCE 16

Jean Monnet (seated) and Robert Schuman, the French ministers who worked to achieve greater co-operation between France, Germany and their neighbours in western Europe.

France and Germany – whose rivalries had been at the root of both world wars. After 1949 it was clear that the two countries would co-operate one day in the NATO alliance (see page 100). However, to reinforce military co-operation it was important to achieve closer industrial and trading links. A useful framework already existed in a committee, the Organisation for European Economic Co-operation (OEEC), which distributed the American Marshall Aid. The experience of OEEC officials showed that it was difficult for countries to rebuild their industries successfully on their own. In 1950 two French ministers, Jean Monnet and Robert Schuman, suggested joining together the coal and steel regions of France and Germany to make them more efficient and profitable.

It was a move for peace as well as profit. Coal and steel are essential to war-making; uniting the French and German coal and steel regions would make future conflict between the two virtually impossible. Other coal-producing countries showed an interest in the scheme, and in 1951 the European Coal and Steel Community (ECSC) was formed. This merged the industries of Italy, Belgium, the Netherlands and Luxembourg as well as those of France and West Germany. The ECSC got off to a flying start. Coal output rose and the production of steel went up by 25 per cent in the first three years. This was partly a result of the increased demand for steel caused by the Korean war.

Britain did not join the ECSC. At the time the country was producing half of all western Europe's coal and a third of its steel. The Government felt that Britain was strong enough industrially to 'go it alone'. Furthermore, trading links with the empire were still of great importance to Britain. To the Conservatives, who regained power under Churchill in 1951, it was unthinkable that Britain should turn its back on the empire to join a European union (Source 18). To many Labour supporters, the ECSC was a capitalist organisation which would seek to increase profits at the expense of workers' welfare (Source 19). However, as it turned out, such objections to closer ties with Europe soon began to lose their force.

The European Coal and Steel Community

The same six countries set up the European Economic Community (EEC).

SOURCE 17

Celebrating European co-operation: the first train to carry coal across the frontier between France and Luxembourg after the start of the European Coal and Steel Community (February 1953).

SOURCE 18

Anthony Eden, Britain's Foreign Minister, summed up the Conservative Party's attitude to Europe in January 1952.

This (joining in European co-operation) is something which we know in our bones, we cannot do ... For Britain's story and her interests lie beyond the Continent of Europe. Our thoughts move across the seas to many communities in which our people play their part, in every corner of the world. That is our life: without it we should be no more than some millions of people living on an island off the coast of Europe.

SOURCE 19

A former Labour Chancellor of the Exchequer, Hugh Dalton, explains his party's attitude towards Britain joining any European union.

We were determined not to allow interference by a European Committee with our full employment policy, our social services, our nationalised industries, or our national planning ... No Socialist Party [such as Labour] ... could accept a system by which important parts of national policy were surrendered to a ... European authority, since such an authority would have a permanent anti-Socialist majority and would arouse the hostility of European workers.

Britain joins Europe

The success of the ECSC surprised British politicians. They had not expected France and West Germany to work together so well. Growing prosperity in western Europe soon encouraged the leaders of 'the Six' to form a closer union. In 1957 they founded the European Economic Community (EEC), which was generally known as the Common Market. By the terms of a treaty signed in Rome, the member-states of the EEC agreed to form a free-trading area by gradually removing all tariffs (customs duties) on trade amongst themselves. Duties would still be imposed on trade with countries outside the Community. The Six also agreed to work towards common policies on nuclear energy, agriculture, transport and social welfare, and they looked forward to eventual political union.

Part of the EEC's success stemmed from the swift recovery of West Germany from the effects of war. The Germans had advantages over most of their neighbours. They had no expensive colonies and virtually no armed forces to maintain. They were also forbidden to develop nuclear weapons. Consequently resources could be concentrated on rebuilding industries, transport systems and the ruined cities, which rose from the ashes much quicker than expected. Britain, on the other hand, was burdened with expensive overseas commitments and had to maintain large military forces. The British also tried to keep their 'great power' status by spending large sums on developing nuclear weapons. The future for Britain was clearly not going to be easy **(Source 21)**.

By the 1960s Britain's industrial performance was lagging well behind that of the EEC countries. As a result people's living standards were rising faster on the Continent than in Britain. Furthermore, as the empire shrank and Britain's colonial trade declined, trade with Europe increased rapidly – despite EEC tariff barriers against outsiders. Growing numbers of both Conservative and Labour supporters were changing their minds about joining Europe.

SOURCE 20

In West Germany modern cities soon rose from the ashes and rubble of war. This photograph shows Frankfurt in 1961.

SOURCE 22

Speaking to journalists in Paris, the French President, Charles de Gaulle, says 'Non' to Britain's first attempt to join the Common Market (14 January 1963).

SOURCE 21

Writing in 1952, Leopold Amery, a former Secretary of State for the Colonies in the 1920s, had this to say about Britain's future.

We are face to face with ... a new type of unity ... in the world's affairs ... On the one side [is] the mass production of the United States. On the other hand, we have [in Europe] another great unit of 400,000,000 people ... There are only two alternatives ... [Possibly] Britain will have to be absorbed inside the European Economic Union, while the Dominions (such as Canada and Australia) gravitate (move towards) the great American Union ... The other alternative is [for] the Empire to get together effectively in order to make more use of its resources.

During the 1960s successive British governments applied to join the EEC. Such applications were not welcomed by all member-states. Some Europeans resented the fact that Britain had refused to join in 1957. Others felt that Britain's continuing links with the Commonwealth and its claim to have a 'special relationship' with the USA meant it would be a disruptive influence within Europe. For some years France blocked Britain's entry. But eventually talks began in earnest following the election of Edward Heath's Conservative government in 1970. Britain finally turned the tide of history and became a full member of the European Community, along with the Irish Republic and Denmark, on 1 January 1973.

Hitler had united Europe briefly by conquest. His ambitions had been defeated at a terrible cost. Now Europe set off on a peaceful path to union, one which promised a brighter future for its peoples.

Assessment tasks

A Knowledge and understanding

1 The first cartoon on this page appeared at the time of the Beveridge Report (1942), the others after the official beginning of Britain's Welfare State in 1948. Describe the ideas and attitudes behind each cartoon.

2 Here are some possible causes of the decline of the British empire.
 • American disapproval of colonial rule
 • Britain being in debt and weakened by the war
 • The campaign in India against British rule
 • The involvement of colonial troops in the Second World War
 • Labour's election victory in 1945
 a Which do you think was the most important, and why?
 b How are these causes linked?

3 When the EEC was formed, a leading Belgian politician said he feared it would dissolve 'like a lump of sugar in a British cup of tea' if Britain joined.
 a What attitudes in Britain might have justified this remark?
 b What factors later caused some of these British attitudes to change?

B Interpretations and sources

4 Here are two contrasting views of the benefits or otherwise of belonging to the EEC (now called the European Union).

> Out of the almost ruined civilisation of 1945 ... most of Europe west of the river Elbe has, for the first time in history, joined in a voluntary association for the sake of peace and prosperity ... The greatest achievement of the EEC has been the progressive lowering of barriers ... between the member states ... Some 50 per cent of their total trade is with other member states. Even the United Kingdom now does over 42 per cent of its trade with its EEC partners.
> (G.N. Minshull, 1985)

> This whole idea of 'Europe' has never been anything other than a gigantic act of make believe ... When Edward Heath ... [took Britain in] it became clear that the sole purpose of the Market was to ensnare ... the British people into a ludicrous web of VAT regulation, put up the price of their food, fill their roads with juggernauts ... and finally, to add injury to insult, filch (steal) all our fish from the North Sea.
> (C. Booker, 1980)

 a Can you account for the differences between these views?
 b Which view do you find the more convincing, and why?

5 Re-read Sources 2, 4, and 5. How far do they help to explain: (a) the surprise at Churchill's election defeat, and (b) the reasons for this defeat?

6 The views expressed in Sources 18 and 19 reflect the official policies of the Conservative and Labour parties at the time. Does this make them more or less useful to historians? Give reasons for your answer.

THE WELFARE STATE

Glossary

ATS Auxiliary Territorial Service – a women's organisation attached to the British Army.

Anderson shelter Metal bomb shelter a family could put up in its garden. Named after Sir John Anderson, a British government minister before the war.

Annexation Forcible takeover of the territory of another country.

Anschluss Union of Austria and Germany, forced by Hitler in 1938.

Appeasement Attempt to pacify an opponent and avoid war.

ARP Air Raid Precautions – the system of civil defence in Britain during the war.

BEF British Expeditionary Force – army sent to France in 1939 and rescued from Dunkirk in 1940.

Blackshirts Fascist or Nazi party members, named after the colour of their uniform.

Blitzkrieg German for 'lightning war' – the tactics used against Poland and France. Shortened to Blitz to describe German air attacks on Britain.

Bolsheviks Political group which seized power in Russia in 1917; later known as Communists.

Capitalism System whereby a country's 'capital' – its land, industries, transport, communications, banking etc – is privately owned by individuals and companies.

Chancellor German or Austrian name for prime minister.

Cheka Russian secret police founded by Lenin.

Cold War Rivalry and political confrontation between Communist Russia and the Western Allies, from 1945.

Collectives State-run farms set up in Russia in the 1930s.

Collective security League of Nations scheme whereby if a member-state was attacked by an aggressor other members would come to its aid. It failed when first China, then Abyssinia, were attacked in the 1930s.

Communism System under which private ownership of land, industry, banks etc is replaced by state ownership – usually as a result of armed revolution. Also known as socialism, although socialists generally believe in pursuing their aims by political means.

Congress Assembly or parliament of representatives, usually elected to debate and pass laws, as in the USA.

Conscription Enforced recruitment into the armed forces or to do war work.

Covenant Document setting out policies and principles, as in the Covenant of the League of Nations.

D-Day Start of the Allied invasion of Europe, 6 June 1944; the 'D' stood for deliverance.

Democracy System of government based on discussion and debate in which the people as a whole have a say, particularly by electing representatives at regular intervals.

Demilitarisation Removal of troops and military installations from a region, as in the Rhineland (1919–36).

Depression A sharp decline in trade and industrial production resulting in mass unemployment.

Dictatorship Rule by one person, usually with little concern for public opinion; a one-party state without free elections.

ECSC European Coal and Steel Community.

EEC European Economic Community – widely known as 'the Common Market', subsequently called the EC (European Community) and now known as the European Union.

Fascism Aggressive, racist political movement founded in Italy in the 1920s.

FAO Food and Agriculture Organisation – an agency of the United Nations.

Final Solution Name given by the Nazis to their attempt to wipe out all Jews.

Gestapo Nazi secret police.

Holocaust The slaughter of six million Jews and others in Nazi death camps during the war.

Iron Curtain Dividing line between the Russian-dominated Communist countries and the rest of Europe during the Cold War.

Kaiser German emperor

Kamikaze Japanese suicide plane; an aircraft packed with explosives which the pilot directed at the target and from which he could not escape.

LDV Local Defence Volunteers, renamed the Home Guard; Britain's volunteer civil defence force during the war.

Luftwaffe German air force.

Marshall Plan American financial and material aid to Europe to assist recovery from the war. Named after General George Marshall who supervised it.

'Mein Kampf' Book written by Hitler about his life and ideas; the words mean 'My Struggle'.

Nationalisation Takeover of privately-owned industry by the state.

National Socialist Party Official name of the Nazis, *although in fact they did not favour socialist principles.

NATO North Atlantic Treaty Organisation – a military alliance of Western countries to resist Communist expansion.

OEEC Organisation for European Economic Co-operation, set up originally to distribute Marshall Aid.

Pact An agreement or alliance between countries.

Panzers German tank formations – from the German word for armour.

PLUTO Pipeline Under the Ocean – laid to supply fuel to the Allied armies in Normandy (1944).

Proletariat Working-class or wage-earning people, a word often used by Communists.

Putsch German word for armed rising.

Radar Radio detection and ranging – the location of distant objects, including aircraft and submarines, by rebounding radio waves.

Reichstag German parliament.

Reparations Compensation paid by one country to another for damage caused during a war.

Republic Country without a monarch, usually with a president as head of state.

SS Schutz Staffel – German for Protective Squad, the most powerful element in the Nazi police.

Socialism See Communism.
Soviet A workers' or soldiers' council or congress in Communist Russia.
Swastika Badge of the Nazi party.
Tariffs Customs duties imposed on foreign trade.
Truce Temporary end to warfare; also known as an armistice.
Truman Doctrine President Truman's policy of offering help to any country threatened by Communist aggression.
U-boats German submarines.
UNESCO United Nations Educational, Scientific and Cultural Organisation.
UNICEF United Nations International Children's Emergency Fund.
UNO United Nations Organisation.

USSR Union of Soviet Socialist Republics – the official name of Communist Russia.
V1, V2 German flying bomb (V1) and exploding rocket (V2) aimed at the London area; the 'V' stood for vengeance (for Allied bombing of Germany).
WAAF Women's Auxiliary Air Force.
Warsaw Pact Military alliance formed by Russia and its Communist neighbours to counter NATO.
Welfare State System of social security for all and improved health care, housing and education, set up in Britain during and after the war.
WHO World Health Organisation – an agency of the United Nations.
WRNS Women's Royal Naval Service.
Zionism Movement to achieve a Jewish state in Palestine.

Index

Topics in the National Curriculum Orders are in bold type.
Page numbers in *italics* refer to illustrations.